JUDY GARLAND

JUDY GARLAND

A Pyramid Illustrated History of the Movies

by
JAMES JUNEAU

General Editor: **TED SENNETT**

PUBLICATIONS
NEW YORK

JUDY GARLAND
A Pyramid Illustrated History of the Movies

Copyright © 1974 by Pyramid Communications, Inc.

First edition published July, 1974

ISBN 0-515-03482-7

Library of Congress Catalog Card Number: 74-1569

Pyramid Illustrated History of the Movies

Printed in the United States of America

Pyramid Books are published by Pyramid Communications, Inc. Its trademarks, consisting of the word "Pyramid" and the portrayal of a pyramid, are registered in the United States Patent Office.

Pyramid Communications, Inc., 919 Third Avenue, New York, N.Y. 10022

(graphic design by anthony basile)

ACKNOWLEDGMENTS

My thanks to Charles Silver and Stephen Harvey, Film Study Center, Museum of Modern Art; Films Incorporated; Patrick Sheehan and Joe Balian, Library of Congress; The Echo Book Shop; Miles Kreuger, The Institute of the American Musical; Howard Mandelbaum and Roger McNiven, The Thousand Eyes; Jerry Vermilye and William Pratt for providing the photographs; and, especially, Ed Kennebeck.

CONTENTS

Is there an adult American who as a child was not taken to see *The Wizard of Oz*? Is there an American child today who can escape the periodic television showings of this film? *The Wizard of Oz* and Judy Garland herself are practically federally sanctioned. Other Garland films are likely to show up on television during holidays, and it would probably be as easy to find a child who hasn't heard of Santa Claus as one who hasn't heard of Judy. Late in her life, mocking her preposterous fame, Garland would compare herself to the Statue of Liberty; the comparison was apt.

Garland began her nationwide wooing of the public on radio in 1935, when she was only twelve years old. There were periods of inactivity, but through radio, movies, the concert stage, recordings, night clubs, and television, she achieved a continuity in a love affair with the public that she never could achieve in her private life. She made retreats from public notice, but their effect was similar to the one she obtained by the calculated late arrivals for her concert appearances: mounting suspense in the audience while she held fire in the wings. It made possible for audiences the ritual pleasures of the frequent "comebacks." As a national resource Judy Garland was not permitted periods of rest and retirement. Retreat was failure; a

INTRODUCTION

resumption of work, a glorious comeback. Certainly no entertainer was ever welcomed back so often.

Hardly a year had elapsed since her ignominious departure from Metro-Goldwyn-Mayer in 1950, when she staged her first comeback at London's Palladium, followed by the first "real" one when she in fact "came home" to the Palace in New York.

While she performed with greatest intensity in concert appearances, it was as a contract player for MGM from 1935 to 1950 that the public made the acquaintance of Judy Garland in roles tailored not to offend the taste of Louis B. Mayer, the head of production at the world's largest stable of glamour. If at MGM Garbo was Sin, Garland was Absolution. As one of a constellation of stars ("More stars than there are in heaven," the studio boasted) that contained Garbo, Gable, Turner, and Lamarr, Garland represented the idealized image of the girl next door. Only one of her twenty-seven feature films at Metro was ever "in trouble"—so to speak—with the Legion of Decency. and that was

11

Andy Hardy's doing. When *Life Begins for Andy Hardy* failed to measure up to Decency standards, Metro acceded to the Legion's objections and deleted the offending footage. The clean slate was maintained. In its listings, the organization carefully noted that the A-1 rating (morally unobjectionable for general patronage) applied only to the revised version of the film.

Purity was not the only thing Mayer insisted upon; Garland pictures frequently carried the "message" that there's no place like home, whether home was Kansas, St. Louis or the Caribbean. It is no wonder that when she slipped away from her MGM overlords, Judy Garland—who took five husbands and died an early death at forty-seven in 1969—lived a private life that probably would have drawn a B rating from the Legion—morally objectionable in part for all. Occasionally in literature, a fictional character detaches himself from the work that gave him life and takes on an independent existence. (Sherlock Holmes is a clear example.) But this process is routine for movie stars. The power of the visual image is so immense that one actor appearing in a succession of roles can accumulate great impact. Hortense Powdermaker, in *Hollywood: The Dream Factory*, observes: "When the average movie-goer describes a pic-

ture he has seen, he gives the plot in terms of what happened to John Garfield, Bing Crosby or Ingrid Bergman."* Judy Garland played many characters with many different names, but we finally perceive "Judy Garland" as if she were herself a fictional character.

The tendency to see stars as figures in a myth is also reinforced and confirmed by a tendency to turn these stars *into* fiction. Before her girl-next-door image had given way, Judy was a character in one of a quaint movie star "sleuth" series printed on war-rationed paper. The segment in which she figured was called *Judy Garland and the Hoodoo Costume*. Toward the end of Garland's career, after the private life had become public domain, we were given Jacqueline Susann's version of her in *Valley of the Dolls*. It was common knowledge that she was the model for the emotionally disturbed, pill-ridden Neely, just as the promoters of that book intended. In a weak moment Garland came close to countenancing this exploitation by agreeing to appear in the film of the novel. She was not slated to play Neely, but a marginal role that subsequently went to Susan Hayward. Another example of Garland being turned into fiction is a pulp

*Hortense Powdermaker, *Hollywood: The Dream Factory*, Little, Brown, Boston, 1950, p. 207.

13

Costume test for
VALLEY OF THE DOLLS (1967)

novel called *Julie*. It portrays one "Julie Goodman," who not only "sang like a bird"—according to the cover copy—but also "turned into a prowling tigress with fire in her loins that demanded daily quenching." On the inside of the book, the disclaimer reading "resemblance to persons living or dead is purely coincidental" is in unusually bold type.

The Judy of the twenty-seven MGM features (and one loan-out to 20th Century-Fox) is spunky, independent, vulnerable, self-deprecating, mocking, wry, witty, romantic, affecting, and—especially —wide open and accessible. She never held an audience at arm's length; instead her performances made each viewer feel as if he were brought up close. Her talent for reaching an audience was made tangible in concert appearances; fans rushed the stage for the ritual touching of hands which often concluded a Garland performance.

Garland's singing talent brought her to the attention of MGM. It was the full-throated voice that made Louis B. Mayer sign up a pudgy twelve-year-old without the bother of a screen test. But Garland was an accomplished actress as well and a brilliant natural comedienne, farceur and clown. Her full capabilities as a dramatic actress were seldom exploited by the studio, which may explain why she sought other outlets for this, such as the performance of *Alice Adams* on radio. Whether she appeared in a comedy or a drama, the script always provided an occasion for her to shed tears. (In *Summer Stock* even the wreckage of a tractor sets her off.) Frequently, she would shed tears while continuing to chatter and fight them back. At the same time no one in films possessed a laugh as infectious and true as hers. And usually Garland was laughing at herself.

Garland made real the cliché about singing one's way into the hearts of millions. The memory of Garland as Dorothy was so immediate and vivid—even after she had taken a fifth husband—that everything afterwards that happened to Garland happened to Dorothy as well.

17

One should resist saying that Judy Garland was born in a trunk, but it might almost be accurate, at least metaphorically. She was the daughter of parents with show-business aspirations. At ten her father, Frank Avent Gumm, had run away from Murfreesboro, Tennessee, to join a minstrel show. Several years later he was the tenor who led audiences in songfests between shows at a movie theater in Superior, Wisconsin. The piano player was Ethel Marian Milne, who was Irish like him, and, also like him, loved show business. They teamed up professionally and matrimonially. As Jack and Virginia Lee, Sweet Southern Singers, they played vaudeville—a long way from the Keith-Orpheum circuit. As Mr. and Mrs. Frank Gumm, they produced two daughters, Sue in 1916, and Virginia in 1919.

This family expansion immobilized the Gumms. They settled in Grand Rapids, Michigan, where Frank managed a local theater. Ethel coached Sue and Virginia in singing, and formed an act. It was during this period of comparative stability that Ethel gave birth to Frances Ethel Gumm on June 10, 1922. Years later, of course, Frances would be known as Judy Garland.

Ethel continued the coaching, but it "took" with only her youngest daughter. According to hard-to-

A GUMM SISTER BECOMES JUDY GARLAND

substantiate legend, this third daughter made her stage debut at two and a half. It was Christmas week of 1924. Accounts of Frances Gumm's debut have as many variant readings as there are "reporters" of the event. These stories may possess elements of truth, even though each writer seems to add his own embroidery. What is unvarying in the accounts are two older Gumm Sisters singing onstage, Baby Frances present in the theater, and her sudden appearance onstage to sing, unprodded, choruses of "Jingle Bells." In some accounts she bolts out of the lap of her grandmother, who sits in the audience; in others her grandmother *releases* her from her lap and pushes her toward the stage; in others grandmother *carries* her to the stage; others stand grandmother in the wings, and there are even accounts which leave grandmother totally out of the picture. Depending upon whom you credit, Frances's lungs got her through anywhere from two to fifteen choruses of "Jingle Bells" before she was carried off. It is one of the key events in Garland folklore, and it could even be true.

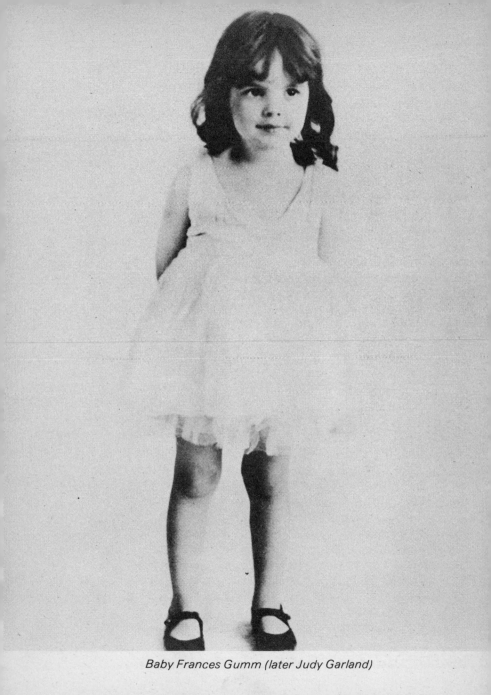

Baby Frances Gumm (later Judy Garland)

Nonetheless, Frances was the first of the Gumm sisters to show any real sparks of talent. This recognition, and the ascendency of the child actor in Hollywood—Jackie Coogan and Chaplin's *The Kid* had happened in 1921—may have emboldened Ethel to suggest to Frank that they give up Grand Rapids for Hollywood. They sold their house and left for Hollywood in the summer of 1924. Many years later, writing for *McCall's*, Garland remembered the exodus from Minnesota: "We all piled into our old touring car and spent three months on the road, playing one-night stands in just about every city between Grand Rapids and Los Angeles." (This trek west must have roughly coincided with one made out of Kansas City by Nell Carter Yule and her preschool child, Joe, Jr. Mrs. Yule also had a history of vaudeville appearances in tank towns, and she was making the journey to get her boy parts in Hal Roach comedies. It seemed worth the trouble of sleeping under a lean-to and cooking out-of-doors until they hit Hollywood, especially after Joe Yule, Jr. had changed his name to Mickey Rooney.)

The Gumms lived in Los Angeles for six months while Frank scouted for a theater. He found one in Lancaster, a desert town eighty miles from Los Angeles. With a father who managed a movie theater,

Frances was able to grow up watching movies. She continued to sing with her sisters, but since she was still of preschool age and her sisters were in school, her mother would take her to Los Angeles and book her as a single, playing "theaters, luncheons, whatever." Ethel often traveled as far as Seattle to secure bookings.

Before the move to Lancaster, Ethel had signed up the Gumm Sisters with the Meglin Kiddies, a booking agent for child acts. It is possible that Frances Gumm and her sisters appeared in shorts produced by Vitagraph with the Meglin Kiddies.

In 1932 Ethel decided it was time for a direct assault on Hollywood. She again persuaded Frank to make a move, this time, right into Los Angeles. Frank bought a theater in Lomita; Ethel enrolled Frances in Miss Lawlor's School for Professional Children. At the school one of Frances's classmates was a boy called Mickey McGuire. He was Mickey Rooney, formerly Joe Yule, Jr., in the middle stage of his evolution. Of the Lawlor School, Rooney later wrote succinctly: "No child ever broke down under the study load." Ethel was not opposed to keeping Frances out of school if a booking came along.

About this time, things started to happen for Ethel and Frances. Loading the Gumm Sisters into

20

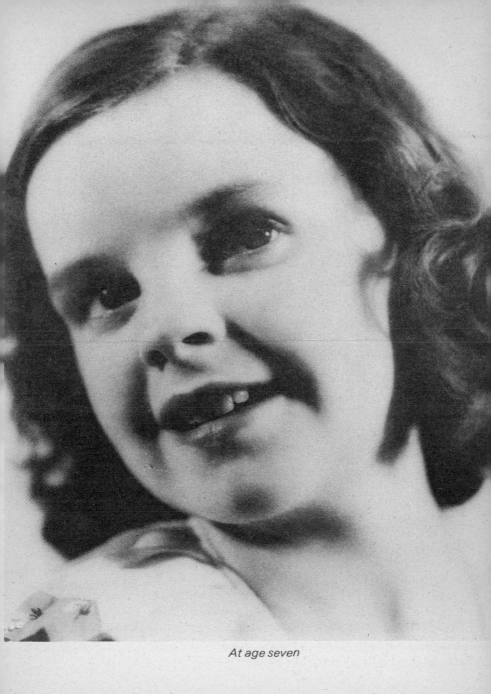

At age seven

As a young girl

their touring car—and leaving Frank behind—Ethel drove to Denver. The Gumm Sisters played there for a week, and moved on to Chicago. The Gumms were booked into the Century of Progress Exhibition at the 1933 Chicago World's Fair. This led to another Chicago booking at the Oriental Theatre, and to the second key event in the Garland saga: How Judy Got Her Name.

George Jessel was the headliner on the bill. The story goes that the Gumms, arriving at the Oriental, found their name misspelled on the marquee as The Glum Sisters. Jessel comforted the distressed Gumms, and observed that their real name wasn't much of an improvement. Thinking of his friend, drama critic Robert Garland of the New York *World-Telegram*, he proposed his friend's last name. Shortly afterwards, Frances, who was called "Baby" by everyone, discarded her own first name and assumed "Judy" after the Hoagy Carmichael-Sam Lerner song.

In 1934, the Gumms were winding up a four-week run at the Cal-Neva Lodge at Lake Tahoe. It was their second summer there. The owner of the lodge asked Judy to sing for some of his friends. The "friends" were Lew Brown, casting director for Columbia Pictures; Harry Akst, the songwriter; and Al Rosen, a Hollywood agent. For this audition Judy sang "Dinah," which Akst had composed. Rosen slipped his phone number into Judy's hand and told her to have her mother call him in Los Angeles.

Akst became Judy's first agent. He took her around to the big studios, but without success. One day, a call came from Rosen to come to MGM for an audition. Here is how Judy recalled it:

"Daddy played a little piano, and I sang for Jack Robbins, the Metro talent chief. I sang 'Zing! Went The Strings of My Heart.' He called in Ida Koverman, Louis B. Mayer's secretary. They called in Roger Edens, who was the rehearsal piano player for the lot at the time. He had been with Ethel Merman in New York, and he played 'Zing!' better than my father. But Daddy was beaming, because it was the only time he had a chance to be that kind of father. My face was still dirty, but he was proud of me. Miss Koverman called Louis Mayer to come right down to hear me. When she hung up the phone, she said, 'He's coming!' Like it was the resurrection! I didn't know who he was. My father didn't know either."*

Roger Edens also remembers that historic afternoon:

"Her mother brought Judy to me

*Judy Garland, *"There'll Always Be an Encore,"* McCall's, January, 1964, p. 141.

23

At age twelve

to audition. Her mother played the piano and she sang 'Zing! Went the Strings of My Heart.' I knew instantly, in eight bars of music. The talent was that inbred. She sang it exactly as she sings it today, her mother's arrangement. I fell flat on my face . . . I called Ida Koverman, L.B. Mayer's secretary, and she called Mr. Mayer, and he called the lawyers and she was signed to a contract that day. It was like discovering gold at Sutter's Creek. Mayer took her all over the lot that day and made her sing for everyone."*

So much for eyewitness accounts. Nonetheless, both versions jibe in the crucial details. Perhaps Judy, whose father was to die of spinal meningitis in only a few months, was spinning a fantasy that enabled her to make him a part of her new life at MGM. Ethel continued to exert her will over Judy, and, in some sense, Louis B. Mayer stepped into the place left vacant by her father. Or perhaps Roger Edens has imperfect memory. At any rate, they convey the impact and the rarity of a twelve-year-old talent like Judy Garland.

Two weeks later Judy reported for work at MGM. Edens worked with her for two hours a day, six days a week; "never on scales, just singing and working on the ar-

*James Goode, "Judy," *Show Business Illustrated*, October 31, 1961, p. 44.

rangements that I wrote for her," Edens explained. Because of her age, Judy was also required by law to spend three hours each day in the MGM school, where Mickey Rooney, Deanna Durbin, Jackie Cooper, and Freddie Bartholomew—all future co-stars—were also enrolled.

Metro didn't know how to showcase Judy's talent, so it was over a year before she made a movie for them. She was introduced on the radio in 1935, becoming practically a regular on "The Bob Hope Show." She also sang at dinners and parties given by the studio. Finally, the studio did test her with Deanna Durbin. Judy described it as "sort of on Jazz versus Opera. I had an apple in my hand and a dirty face, and she was the Princess of Transylvania or some crazy thing."

As a follow-up to this test, the two girls were teamed in a one-reeler, *Every Sunday*. Felix E. Feist, who specialized in shooting short subjects for the studio, was assigned to direct. Con Conrad and Herb Magidson, composers of "The Continental," wrote a complementary song for this film called "Americana." It was as appropriate to Judy as "The Continental" was to Astaire and Rogers.

Every Sunday is a charming featherweight, all the future Mickey-and-Judy-Let's-Put-on-a-Show films in capsule. The bandshell concerts that Durbin's grandfather puts

25

EVERY SUNDAY (1936). With Deanna Durbin

EVERY SUNDAY (1936). With Deanna Durbin

on every Sunday are being halted by the villainous town council because of poor attendance. Durbin (called by her real name, Edna, in the film) and her friend Judy decide to take action to avert this tragedy. They spend a week campaigning and drumming up business for next Sunday's concert, painting signs and making door-to-door solicitations. On Sunday the girls escort Granddad to the poorly attended concert, where Durbin mounts the platform to sing. Idlers in the park, hearing her, come running. Then Judy mounts the stage and delivers

the rousing "Americana," exhorting everyone to "dance and make love to the music of Americana." She keeps accelerating the pace, and by the time Durbin has joined her to sing counterpoint, the audience has swelled and the town council villains have been thwarted.

The film reveals how confident and accomplished a performer Judy Garland already was at fourteen. She looks as if an MGM scout had plucked her off a farm, and there is an irresistible sincerity and eagerness to please in her singing and acting. The contrast between Dur-

27

PIGSKIN PARADE (1936). With Tony Martin and Dixie Dunbar

bin and Garland goes beyond the former singing in "classy" style —with her elbows sticking out like wings and the fingers of both hands interlocked—and the latter singing "swing." Durbin is well-groomed, stiff and polite, but Garland has all the vitality.

This was a beginning for Judy, but still no one at MGM could come up with a way to present a slightly pudgy, fourteen-year-old-singer. The studio took the cowardly way out, and loaned her to 20th Century-Fox for her first feature. (20th Century had been founded on money provided by Mayer and Nicholas Schenck, and Schenck, president of Loew's Inc., the parent company of MGM, was the brother of Fox's head of production.)

Even for a movie *designed* not to make sense, *Pigskin Parade* (1936) is pretty silly. Through error a small Texas university's football team is invited to play against Yale. By some absurd machinations, the Texas team actually defeats the Ivy

28

Leaguers. Judy is listed ninth in the credits, after such players as Stuart Erwin, Jack Haley, Betty Grable, Arline Judge, and Dixie Dunbar. This billing doesn't reflect the musical load she was called upon to carry. Most of the singing chores devolved upon her. (One excepts The Yacht Club Boys, a quartet of overage sophomores who sing four of their own compositions, "rah-rah" drinking songs that all sound alike.)

Judy plays the sister of Arkansas yokel Stuart Erwin. Scouts from the Texas football team see the way he pitches watermelon, and figure if he can handle a football as effectively, he'll help out the team. They bring him and his sister back to Texas. When the girl from Arkansas is exposed to the "civilizing" influence of Texas, she changes her name to the sweet-sounding Murine. "I got it offen a bottle," she explains. Like Erwin, who received an Academy Award nomination for best supporting actor, Judy talks with a cumbersome and not very credible hillbilly accent. When she goes before an audience to sing, as she does three times, she steps out of her character to do it.

She belts "The Texas Tornado"

BROADWAY MELODY OF 1938 (1937). With Sophie Tucker and Barnett Parker

from the back of a train departing for New Haven; leads collegiate dancers in the big production number, "The Balboa" and sings the plaintive "It's Love I'm After" to a stadium full of spectators during halftime at the climactic football game.

Patsy Kelly gives the most memorable performance as the wife of Jack Haley, the football coach recruited from back east—Flushing, to be exact. As the assertive partner in their marriage, she whispers plays to him, which he passes on to the team as his own. At a school dance where she has had too much to drink, she ends the evening swinging in the gym on the exercise rings. She also sets the foolish plot in motion by dropping a dumbbell on the team's star player and incapacitating him for the game.

Pigskin Parade was the first and last time Metro permitted Judy Garland to stray off the lot while under contract to them. Her next film, in which she is a featured player, was *Broadway Melody of 1938* (1937). At a party to celebrate Clark Gable's thirty-sixth birthday —February 1, 1937—Judy sang "You Made Me Love You" to the actor. Roger Edens had written special material for the song. At one point in the song, Judy interpolated an ardent testimonial of her love for Gable. Her number was so well received that it was written

into the *Broadway Melody*, another entry in the series used as a catch-all for the musical talent on the lot.

In the number Judy is able to create the character of a lovesick fan. Her rendition is so delicate that she makes it both poignant and funny. One can say of Judy what she says of Gable in the song, that her acting is so "natural-like." She recorded the song for Decca. It was an enormous success, giving her her first important national recognition. "Dear Mr. Gable" brought her one step closer to stardom.

Judy's next film, also made in 1937, is notable only for bringing her together with Mickey Rooney for the first time. Directed by Alfred E. Green, *Thoroughbreds Don't Cry* was a story about horse racing, a subject dear to the heart of Louis B. Mayer, who was soon to set up his own racing stables. Judy played Cricket, a spunky girl who helps a young British lad (Robert Sinclair in a role intended for Freddie Bartholomew) to ride his horse to victory. (Rooney played the jockey.) Judy sang only once: "Got a New Pair of Shoes" by Nacio Herb Brown and Arthur Freed.

Everybody Sing, the first of her three films released in 1938, was hardly a good film, but it was not without its moments. Judy is the central figure, though she is surrounded by an impressive group of thirties players: Fanny Brice, Allan

BROADWAY MELODY OF 1938 (1937). As Betty Clayton

Jones, Billie Burke, Reginald Owen, Monty Woolley, and Reginald Gardiner. This venture into screwball farce was unusual for MGM, which must have been inspired by the success of films like *My Man Godfrey* to offer its own family of eccentrics. The movie is noisy, shrill and silly, but occasionally it works.

Judy is adrift in a household in which everyone is either crazy (Billie Burke, Reginald Owen), a little eccentric (Fanny Brice) or bland (Allan Jones, Lynne Carver). She returns home after being expelled from her third school for singing "swing" music. Her parents, concerned only about the play they are involved in putting on, turn deaf ears to her plight. When someone finally gets through to them, Dad prescribes the Grand Tour. Since this will mean not appearing in the show the family cook (Jones) is putting on, Judy plants someone on the boat to take her place. In an obvious blackface disguise, she auditions for the show, singing "Swing Low, Sweet Chariot." But she gets the job anyway, the show is a hit, and she saves her irresponsible Mom and Dad from impending bankruptcy.

The film opens blissfully in a classroom of the private Colvin School for Girls. A purse-lipped, buttoned-up schoolmistress is leading a class of bored girls in the singing of Mendelssohn's "Spring Song." When she is called away, perky Judy's eyes light up, and by converting the song to a swing rhythm, she brings everybody back alive. She plants her feet firmly on the ground in the stance that would become her trademark and sings, with a clarity and volume that belie her years, "Sing, Mr. Mendelssohn, Sing." Of course, the schoolmistress returns and sends her to the principal's office.

Though her skill as an actress was not fully developed, she betrays none of the precocity of the fastidious enunciation that seem to be occupational hazards for child actors. In these early films she does have a tendency to crinkle up her nose too often—and in *Everybody Sing* she is given the "cute" business of pressing it flat against a window. Since her actor's instinct is so true everywhere else, one wants to blame these excesses on her misguided directors.

Everybody Sing is also valuable for putting Judy, dressed as Little Lord Fauntleroy, opposite Fanny Brice, appearing as "Baby Snooks," in a charming number, "Why? Because!" There is also a stab at a "There's No Business Like Show Business" anthem. It's called "The Show Must Go On" but it doesn't make it.

Edwin L. Marin, who directed *Everybody Sing*, also guided her

32

THOROUGHBREDS DON'T CRY (1937). With Sophie Tucker

EVERYBODY SING (1938). With Allan Jones and Henry Armetta

LISTEN, DARLING (1938). With Mary Astor

LOVE FINDS ANDY HARDY (1938). With Mickey Rooney

through her next picture. (Judy was yet to appear in a film with one of the studio's top directors at the helm.) In *Listen, Darling* (1938), she was teamed with Freddie Bartholomew, whose sensitive manner and air of British rectitude kept him a popular juvenile actor for several years after *David Copperfield*. When Judy's widowed mother (Mary Astor) decides to take a husband for her children's financial security (not for love), Judy and boyfriend Bartholomew abduct her and take her on a cross-country search for a suitable husband. Happily, the search turns up Walter Pidgeon.

Judy sings "Zing! Went the Strings of my Heart," the song that got her hired at MGM, as well as "On the Bumpy Road to Love" and "Tenpins in the Sky."

Love Finds Andy Hardy (1938) was her sixth feature, and the last before she would achieve new status at MGM with the phenomenal success of *The Wizard of Oz*. Louis B. Mayer took a proprietary interest in the Hardy family series, which, with its well-scrubbed, sentimental view of domestic life, apparently reflected his idea of the American dream. It must have also appealed to him for bringing in large returns on modest investments. The Hardy films were also a way of showcasing and developing the considerable number of young actors and actresses under contract. Lana Turner, who is in *Love Finds Andy Hardy*, Donna Reed, Esther Williams, and Kathryn Grayson were among the players who were used in the series at the outset of their careers.

Judy plays Betsy Booth, a visitor to Andy Hardy's home town, Carvel. (Her first lines to Andy are memorable: "Hello!" she says, beaming. "My name is Betsy Booth! I *sing!*") She becomes embroiled in Andy's insoluble problem—which of three girls to take to the big dance. She also gets to prove her opening statement by rendering three songs. Judy would play the same character in two subsequent Hardy pictures.

In 1938 Judy Garland was cast in the role with which she is most identified: Dorothy, the Kansas farm girl lost in Oz. Her singing of "Over the Rainbow" made such an impression that it became her theme song. She couldn't escape it for the rest of her life, much as she tried. When she was shooting her weekly television series in 1963, it was only after much persuasion that she could be coaxed into singing the song on the air, although its melody was 'heard frequently as one of the themes that introduced the show. When she died in 1969, it automatically became, for many, her epitaph. Sob sister eulogists (of either sex) reverently quoted fan declarations that "she's found that rainbow now."

But both this role and this song were almost withheld from her. The money men at the studio wanted Shirley Temple to play Dorothy, although Arthur Freed and Mervyn LeRoy were pushing for Judy. Fox, which had Shirley under contract, was playing hard-to-get. When negotiations seemed to have run aground, the front office acceded to the producers' choice of Garland. That they didn't have much confidence in this choice is suggested by the steps taken by Jack Dawn's makeup department, which worked her over so much that Judy Garland was nearly obliterated with a blonde

OFF TO SEE THE WIZARD

wig, a remodeled nose and caps on her teeth. She probably emerged looking like Vicki Lester after her marathon session in the makeup man's chair in *A Star Is Born*. The inadvisability of this refurbishing was recognized after three weeks of shooting. Production was halted, and it was decided to take Judy Garland as she was.

However, one problem remained. L. Frank Baum doesn't specify the age of his heroine in the first of the Oz books, which he began publishing in 1900, but it is clear that she is probably closer to Miss Temple's age in 1938 (ten) than Miss Garland's in the same year (sixteen). Although Garland's physical development hadn't been especially rapid, there were undeniable breasts and curves and they called for a bit of reupholstering. Dorothy could be no nymphet. A corset flattened out the chest. Prosaic gingham was the fabric the costume department used for the one dress she wears in the film. (Reportedly, Judy went through ten of these during the year's shooting.) And, finally, her hair was put in bows.

There were other preproduction problems. Makeup also had to

37

THE WIZARD OF OZ (1939). With Billie Burke and the Munchkins in Oz

come up with ways to turn Ray Bolger, Jack Haley, and Bert Lahr into credible figures of fantasy: respectively, a scarecrow, a tin man, and a lion. The department had learned the lesson of Paramount's *Alice in Wonderland* back in 1933. The advantage of an all-star cast in that production (Cary Grant as the Mock Turtle, W.C. Fields as Humpty Dumpty, etc.) had been effectively lost by hiding everyone behind masks. The result was a critical and financial disaster. To avert this, the studio had the actors suffer hours in makeup before reporting on the set to face further suffering under the hot lights. Their costumes covered practically their whole bodies, except for the faces, which were heavily made up. The transformation of the actors was artfully achieved.

Casting was also scrupulous. The casting department combed the country for midgets to play Munchkins. It was emphatic about excluding dwarfs and "deformed people" from the ranks of the Munchkins, who were tiny, rotund people who inhabited one area of Oz. Actually, the Munchkins who figured most prominently in the film were members of a veteran vaudeville troupe, Singer's Midgets. (There is talk that some of the Munchkins in positions remote from the camera's eye are really

THE WIZARD OF OZ (1939). With Jack Haley, Ray Bolger, and Bert Lahr

children!) Margaret Hamilton, as the nasty, spiteful Almira Gulch in the Kansas section that frames the Oz story, and later as the Wicked Witch of the West, was a perfect choice, and the makeup department found the ideal shade of sickly green to paint her.

Composer Harold Arlen and lyricist E.Y. Harburg also provided one of the brightest and richest scores ever devised for a musical film. Besides the legendary "Over the Rainbow" there are the infectious "Ding-Dong! The Witch Is Dead," the cheerful "We're Off to See the Wizard," the sprightly "If I Only Had a Brain," and the non-

sensical "If I Were King of the Forest." "Over the Rainbow" was deleted from the film two different times, but was restored at the objections of its composers and Arthur Freed. It was felt by some that the song slowed up the picture. A production number, "The Jitterbug," which involved dancing trees, did get cut from the film.

According to Garland, *Wizard* went through seven directors. It is signed by Victor Fleming, who was pulled off the picture to finish *Gone with the Wind* when George Cukor was fired from that epic. In spite of this, the finished film was successful beyond even the fantasies of Louis

THE WIZARD OF OZ (1939). With Margaret Hamilton

THE WIZARD OF OZ (1939). With Ray Bolger and Jack Haley

B. Mayer. It is probably the most totally successful film Garland ever made, and it made her a major star. Part of the film's success can be attributed to the Baum story, which Noel Langley, Florence Ryerson, and Edgar Allan Woolf followed closely in their screenplay. The story is worked out in terms immediately comprehensible and vivid to children: the fear of getting lost in a strange neighborhood or being separated from parents and home, the terror of falling into the clutches of a hideous old witch who threatens to kill your pet dog.

The decision to use sepia for the realistic scenes in Kansas and color for the fantastic sequences in Oz was a brilliant one. When Dorothy wakes up in the wreckage of her home, which she doesn't yet realize has been pitched by a cyclone from Kansas to Oz, and opens the door for her first look at that wonderland, the effect of the glorious pastels is magical and overwhelming, especially to children. Dorothy's first remark to her dog is a masterpiece of understatement: "Toto, I have a feeling we're not in Kansas any more."

THE WIZARD OF OZ (1939). Dorothy and friends in Emerald City

Clutching Toto, Dorothy takes tentative steps into Oz. Suddenly, a ball of light descends from the heavens and materializes into Glinda the Good Witch (Billie Burke). Since Dorothy's house had landed on top of the Wicked Witch of the East, Glinda warns Dorothy to avoid her surviving sister, the Wicked Witch of the West. She starts her out on the Yellow Brick Road which will lead her to the Wizard of Oz in Emerald City. He alone can show her the way back to Kansas. Along the way Dorothy is joined by the Scarecrow, who wants to ask the Wizard for a brain; by the Tin Woodman, who would like the Wizard to give him a heart, and the Cowardly Lion, who wants to ask him for courage. Together, they have many adventures as they flee from the Wicked Witch, until Dorothy is returned to her beloved Kansas farm, where she exclaims: "There's no place like home!"

As her traveling companions to Oz, Ray Bolger, Jack Haley, and Bert Lahr are so perfect, so artfully winning that they were identified with their roles for many years.

43

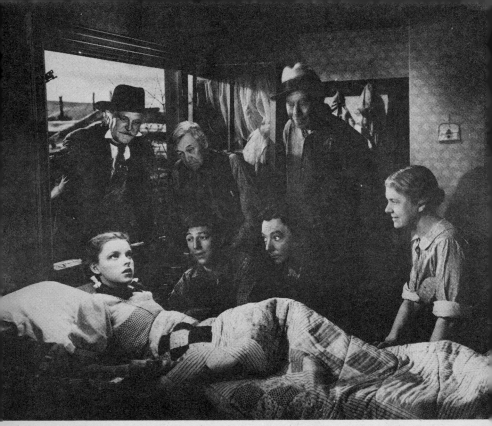

THE WIZARD OF OZ (1939). With (left to right) Frank Morgan, Charley Grapewin, Ray Bolger, Jack Haley, Bert Lahr, and Clara Blandick

Bolger as the Scarecrow, frantically trying to replace some lost stuffing and longing wistfully for a brain, and Haley as the Tin Woodman, oiling his creaking joints and wishing for a heart, were both splendid. For many, however, the edge went to Bert Lahr as the Cowardly Lion. Bellowing in terror, sniveling at the sight of every shadow, he was a wonderfully endearing dethroned King of the Jungle, who finally finds his courage.

Ultimately, however, the decision that was most responsible for the film's success was the one to cast Garland as Dorothy. Her sincerity and that affecting quality she possessed never served a film so well. Whether gently scolding the Lion for making "such a fuss," or confronting the Witch with childish courage, or saying a tearful goodbye to her friends in Oz, she projected a tremulous charm that pleased audiences of all ages. She was awarded a

44

special miniature Oscar for her performance, and found herself at the threshold of a productive decade as MGM's leading musical star.

Nothing is perfect, of course, and one can quibble with the film. It *is* dismaying that what Dorothy finds over the rainbow is positive thinking. The flying monkeys who are in thrall to the Witch are more disturbingly grotesque than necessary. And it is also a letdown for Frank Morgan's Wizard to be exposed as a charlatan. (W.C. Fields, who held out for too much money to play the role, might have been less of a letdown; he could have given the Wizard's good advice a double edge.) Since Dorothy wakes up to discover it's all a dream anyway, it seems we could have been given a real Wizard.

Flaws and all, *The Wizard of Oz* was an enormous success. 20th Century-Fox, hoping to cash in on the struck gold, put into production a color fantasy based on Maurice Maeterlinck's play, *The Blue Bird*. The film was a disaster and, since her ascent to stardom in 1933, the first financial flop for the film's leading player, Shirley Temple.

In addition to a special Academy Award, *The Wizard of Oz* also won Judy Garland an invitation to leave her handprints and signature in the wet cement in front of Grauman's Chinese Theatre. This ritual, enacted on the night of the premiere of her second 1939 hit, *Babes in Arms*, certified her new Hollywood status, and launched the busiest decade of her life. From 1940 to 1950 she reigned as the queen of the musical film. Into this period she crowded twenty feature films and frequent radio and personal appearances.

Garland labored at MGM while the star system was at its peak, and left just as it had begun to erode. Like most of the stars of the thirties and forties, she submitted to the seven-year contract, a form of indentured servitude. It compelled an actor to accept a role or face suspension; to go out on loan to another company at a gain to his studio—but without personal remuneration; and to draw the same paycheck for working six days a week as for sitting idly home waiting for the studio to give you an assignment.

Several years after Garland had left MGM, after Louis B. Mayer, the MGM overlord himself, had been forced out of the company he had helped found, Judy revealed her MGM "horror stories" to the readers of *McCall's*. In them she

DRUDGE IN A DREAM FACTORY

portrayed Mr. Mayer, MGM, and even her late mother as Simon Legrees exploiting their "property" for maximum productivity and profits. In 1964 there was a reprise of some of these stories for the same magazine, along with a few new ones.

Because Judy tended to be chubby, the studio put her on a rigorous diet and enforced it. "From the time I was thirteen," Judy explained, "there was a constant struggle between MGM and me—whether or not to eat, how much to eat, what to eat." The studio commissary was directed to feed her consommé no matter what she ordered; diet pills were prescribed.

Her inventory of injustices also contained this much-quoted passage: "When we were in production, they had us working days and nights on end. They'd give us pep-up pills to keep us on our feet long after we were exhausted. Then they'd take us to the studio hospital and knock us cold with sleeping pills—Mickey sprawled out on one bed, and me on another. Then, after four hours, they'd wake us up and give us the

46

At the premiere of THE GRAPES OF WRATH, with Helen Parrish and Forrest Tucker

pep-up pills again, so we could work another seventy-two hours in a row. Half the time, we were hanging from the ceiling, but it became a way of life for us."*

The exhausting physical and emotional demands of making movies and the inevitable problems of growing up were manifested in her chaotic private life.

And the studio tried to dominate even that. Garland began seeing a psychiatrist in the early forties. When Mayer learned of this, he called a temporary halt. A year later Garland resumed the sessions and continued them for five years.

Mayer even interpreted her first marriage in 1941 to composer David Rose as an encroachment upon his power. About a week after her divorce from Rose in 1945, Judy took Vincente Minnelli as her

*Judy Garland, "There'll Always Be An Encore," *McCall's*, January, 1964 p. 142.

47

second husband. As the studio's top director of musicals, Minnelli was given the Mayer blessing.

Garland even charged that a girl she took as a roommate turned out to be a studio spy. As she grew older, the animosity toward her mother became more open, until it resulted in a permanent rupture and a suit for support filed by her mother the year before she died.

However subjective Garland's account may be, however one-sided—she figures only the debit side of the ledger—it is persuasive by the sheer *amount* of her complaints and by the longevity of her grudge. It is no wonder that she cynically referred to MGM as "the Factory"—Mr. Mayer wouldn't have liked that—and complained that she was overworked and underpaid.

Until the last years at Metro, her performances during the decade give no hint of the behind-the-scenes tensions and headaches. In film after film Garland delivered performances that were intelligent, sensitive, witty, and spontaneous. Not only was she a "fast study," she also needed less rehearsal than most actors. She and Gene Kelly are said to have shot one of her most famous numbers—"Be a Clown" from *The Pirate*—after a mere four hours rehearsal.

Lyricist Arthur Freed, who had

With Vincente Minnelli

been associate producer to Mervyn LeRoy on *Wizard of Oz* and had backed the choice of Judy to play Dorothy from the beginning, became a full-fledged producer and only occasional songwriter with *Babes in Arms* (1939). Freed suggested that Garland and Rooney team up for a musical. The unexpected popularity of the Andy Hardy series had propelled Rooney to stardom. When MGM made the first Hardy picture, *A Family Affair*, in 1937, no series was projected. Overwhelming audience response led to further adventures of the Hardy family, and to the eventual domination of the series by An-

dy. Rooney became one of the biggest moneymakers on the lot. It was clear that Garland was going to be a popular star after the release of *The Wizard of Oz*. In box-office terms, *Babes in Arms* had a lot going for it.

Freed overhauled the Richard Rodgers-Lorenz Hart show, retaining only the title song and "Where or When?" from its score. With his old songwriting partner Nacio Herb Brown, he wrote "Good Morning" especially for the film, and added "I Cried for You," which he'd written with Gus Arnheim, to the score. Harold Arlen and E.Y. Harburg, whose work for *The Wizard of Oz* he had admired, composed the big

BABES IN ARMS (1939). With Mickey Rooney

BABES IN ARMS (1939). With Mickey Rooney and Douglas McPhail

finale, "God's Country." He assigned the script to Jack McGowan and Kay Van Riper, one of the writers of the Hardy pictures.

It is the first of four musicals that Mickey and Judy did over the next five years until Judy moved on to mature roles and Mickey went into the army. The musical is also notable as Busby Berkeley's first full directing chore for Metro after a half-dozen years of musical extravaganzas for Warners.

Mickey and Judy play children of vaudeville. In fact, the birth of the character Mickey plays is announced from the stage of the shrine of vaudeville, the Palace, where his father (Charles Winninger) is appearing. The year is 1921, and the two-a-day is at its peak. We see Mickey's growth through an interpolation of footage from his Mickey McGuire series in the late twenties. The fatal (to vaudeville) advent of the talkies is also represented by clips from two early movie musicals *The Broadway Melody* and *The Hollywood Revue.* The events from 1921 to the time of the film are also filled in by the headlines from *Variety.*

Mickey and Judy are energetic, talented kids, determined to follow in the footsteps of their down-on-their-luck theatrical parents. They are so determined that they are willing to challenge the authority of the town busybody, Miss Steele (Margaret Hamilton, playing another wicked old witch). Miss Steele is equally determined to have the children of Seaport, Long Island, taken away from the corrupt show-business influence and placed in state work schools. The kids *have* to put over that show, to prove their own worth and to save their families from indigence.

Mickey has trouble raising the funds until Baby Rosalie (June Preisser) joins the cast. She is a former child actress interested in making a comeback. Judy, for whom Mickey has written show and songs, must step aside for the noblest reason of all—"the good of the show." On opening night Baby Rosalie doesn't run out on the show in a huff of vanity—as she would have in one of Berkeley's musicals

for Warners, leaving a vacancy for Ruby Keeler to fill. Instead, her father shows up and drags her home by the ear. Judy gets her part back and reclaims Mickey's heart.

Babes in Arms is often exuberant, always naive and unsubtle. In these Mickey-Judy musicals Garland is open, aggressive and eager-to-please. Her eyes never seem to lose their glow of innocence and their sparkle of good cheer. She pitches her whole self into her roles. As her talent matured, she became a more relaxed player. Here she is open and irresistible.

Garland is ebullient singing the spirited "Good Morning," but her high point is the low-key "I Cried for You." She sings it on a rather posh bus speeding her away from Broadway to Schenectady, where she seeks the counsel and wisdom of her mother, after having been rebuffed by Mickey. Her natural dramatic gift enables her to give the song tenderness and humor. Without diminishing the adolescent heartache, she lets us laugh at the multiple clichés she resorts to in order to express that ache.

Rooney, as the youthful entrepreneur, is brash, rambunctious and unself-conscious. He performs with a confidence that could only have come from such a mandate as was implied by his high rank in the popularity polls.

June Preisser is obnoxious in an

51

BABES IN ARMS (1939). The finale of "God's Country"

endearing way as Baby Rosalie, the superannuated child actress who is a parody of Shirley Temple. Spoiled and swell-headed, blonde Baby Rosalie has grown into young womanhood, but she has adopted for life the baby voice and mechanical gestures her dramatic coach taught her. She ingratiates herself from the moment she sits on a stool next to Judy and Mickey, who are drinking coke, and orders sauerkraut juice, "please."

The film's score is pleasant despite the Rodgers and Hart omissions, but the title song is best, used as the springboard for a production number by Berkeley. The defiant kids, forming a united front, sing the song as they stride through the town, picking up more kids as they forge ahead. The number is direct and appealing. However, the finale, "God's Country," is a song only the most mindless patriots could enjoy without

52

ANDY HARDY MEETS DEBUTANTE (1940). With Mickey Rooney

wincing at least once. The message of the song is that it's great to be living in America, "where every man is his own dictator."

This black-and-white film cost a modest $600,000 and grossed over $2,000,000 in the United States alone. Rooney was even nominated for an Oscar for best actor for his performance; he didn't win it, but he did get to present Judy with her special miniature statuette the same year.

The Mickey-Judy combination was now a national resource. They appeared in their next two films together. The first was another in the proliferating Andy Hardy series, *Andy Hardy Meets Debutante* (1940). For the ninth Hardy outing, Andy flirts with a deb (Diana Lewis) until he returns to his constant sweetheart, Polly Benedict (Ann Rutherford). As Betsy Booth again, Judy coaches Andy on how to behave in the company of high

STRIKE UP THE BAND (1940). With Mickey Rooney

society. She also sings the Freed-Brown song, "Alone," and "I'm Nobody's Baby."

Strike Up the Band (1940), the second Mickey-Judy musical, is even hokier than the first. (Busby Berkeley also repeated as director.) It is also interminable. Judy shares star billing with Mickey, but it is really Mickey's show. Some of the sanctimonious sentimentality of the Hardy pictures wound up in this one. Mickey wants to be a band-leader like his idol, Paul White-man. Judy is his classmate at Riverwood High and the girl singer in his high school band. Mickey's attempt to raise the money to get to Chicago for a bandleader contest is thwarted until the end of the picture, just as Mickey is withheld from Judy for the while that teen vamp June Preisser (again) moves in on Mickey.

For a musical with not much on its mind, this film contains a surprising amount of pious advice and self-sacrifice. Ann Shoemaker, as Mickey's mother, enunciates beautifully in the kitchen as she tells her son that she doesn't mind if he doesn't fulfill her dream of his becoming a doctor and becomes a bandleader instead. At another point Mickey sacrifices the two hundred dollars he has finally raised for the Chicago trip so that a young friend can have an important operation. Naturally, this noble act cannot go unrewarded, and it doesn't. It turns out that Paul Whiteman and his orchestra are coming to town to play at a party given by the wealthy parents of Miss Preisser. When the Whiteman group takes its break, Mickey and his men move in on the instruments and audition for the contest then and there. Their success leads to a scene between Mickey and Whiteman who passes down this bit of sage advice: Teach a boy "to blow a horn, and he'll never blow a safe."

Mercifully, Judy provides some relief from all this. She sings "Our Love Affair," which Freed and Roger Edens wrote especially for her for this film. In the melancholy stillness of a library after closing time, she sings "I Ain't Got Nobody," as she broods about the unresponsive Mickey.

With her throaty voice and emotional delivery, Judy seems less like a kid when she starts to sing. She has a bravura number in "La Conga," which Berkeley directs as one of his elaborate set pieces. As a change of pace, he starts it off with Judy singing her solo portion in an unbroken five-minute shot. When the high school dancers join in, Berkeley resumes his typical style of breaking a number into a multiplicity of shots and angles.

It is certainly a much brighter and more infectious number than the flag-waving grand finale —"Strike Up the Band." The number, a barrage of patriotic effects, keeps going long after it should have stopped; it reaches a climax—and the movie ends—on a shot of Mickey and Judy superimposed over the fluttering forty-eight-star American flag.

Freed gave Garland a break from this Mickey-Judy cycle on her next film. Besides restoring her independence, it began the transition from youngster roles to adult ones. The producer had to overcome the resistance of George M. Cohan to obtain *Little Nellie Kelly* as a vehicle for Garland. Cohan didn't make it a practice to sell his work to Hollywood. After obtaining the rights, Freed wasted no undue reverence on the property. Following his usual policy, songs from the original were thrown out and new ones were added. The addition in this case was the Freed-Brown stan-

55

STRIKE UP THE BAND (1940). With William Tracy and Mickey Rooney

dard "Singin' in the Rain." Judy also got to sing "A Pretty Girl Milking Her Cow" and "It's a Great Day for the Irish."

Garland plays a dual role; a mother who dies in childbirth and the grown-up child of that birth. It is also the only time Garland died in a film, although the dual role has almost the effect of a retraction. George Murphy plays the father of Little Nellie Kelly (Garland), and Charles Winninger is Nellie's maternal grandfather. Norman Taurog, who had jerked tears and dollars from movie patrons with his nephew Jackie Cooper in *Skippy*, was the director.

Garland doesn't dominate her next film, *Ziegfield Girl* (1941), even though she is billed above her two glamorous co-stars, Hedy Lamarr and Lana Turner. (James Stewart, with *Destry Rides Again*, *Mr. Smith Goes to Washington*, and an Oscar for *The Philadelphia Story* right behind him, gets billed over all of them.) To balance the elaborate Ziegfeldian numbers in the film, the plot line concentrates on the backstage problems of a trio of fresh recruits to the Follies, three girls who are clearly meant to be "representative."

In terms of a move to more mature roles, *Ziegfeld Girl* is something of a relapse for Garland. Her love interest is the freckle-faced and callow Jackie Cooper, with

LITTLE NELLIE KELLY (1940). With George Murphy

whom the script demands she sip sodas through a straw. Garland's dramatic involvement is with her fading vaudevillian father (Charles Winninger). While she moves up to the Follies, her father breaks up their act and goes out on the circuits. When Judy becomes a big Follies star, she gets her dad invited to do his act there, too.

They do a charming salute to vaudeville in "Laugh? I Could Have Split My Sides," which is a number that makes Ziegfeld scout Noble Sage (Edward Everett Horton) decide he wants Judy for the Follies. Judy also does a big production number, "Minnie from Trinidad." ("She isn't good but she isn't bad.") It was written for her by Roger Edens; Busby Berkeley directed the spectacular sequence. As a Ziegfeld girl, Judy was made to dress in some uncharacteristic get-ups.

As is often the case with Garland, her best moments call for just a camera and a song. For this film it is her rendition of "I'm Always Chasing Rainbows" for her Follies audition. At first she sings it at a fast clip, as her father had insisted. The producers aren't interested, but Lamarr steps in and persuades them to give her another chance. She delivers it this time the way

ZIEGFELD GIRL (1941). With Paul Kelly and Lana Turner (at head of line)

ZIEGFELD GIRL (1941). With Charles Winninger, Paul Kelly, Edward Everett Horton, and Jackie Cooper

her instincts tell her, and makes it a warm, lovely ballad. Everyone is suddenly entranced and Garland is in.

Most of the movie's footage, however, goes to Lana Turner, even though Garland does wind up the only successful Ziegfeld girl of the trio. The moral fable involving Turner must have been dear to the hearts of Mayer *and* the Legion of Decency *and* the Production Code. Turner plays Sheila Regan, a red-headed elevator operator from Flatbush with a devoted truck-driver beau, Jimmy Stewart. The bid from Mr. Ziegfeld turns Sheila's gorgeous head, and she repudiates her family and friends in Flatbush.

As a Ziegfeld girl, Sheila plays the game according to the books. By acquiescing to the suggestions of the stage-door johnnies, she reaps the traditional rewards— minks and a Park Avenue flat. The script puts Sheila through a lot: a worldly rise; dalliance with a millionaire; rupture with Stewart who falls into bad company and goes to jail; moral and physical dissipation; expulsion from the Follies for drinking on the job; pangs of conscience; rapprochement with Stewart and family; heart failure; death; and, by implication, ultimate Ziegfeld glorification in heaven. Mother Courage doesn't have that much baggage to haul.

Before her demise, the film's

60

ZIEGFELD GIRL (1941)._
Judy at the head of the chorus

LIFE BEGINS FOR ANDY HARDY (1941). With Mickey Rooney

finale rounds up all the principal actresses for a Follies opening. Judy is headlining the show; Lamarr, no longer with the Follies, is secure in her box seat with the husband who objected to a working wife; and Turner watches from her pathetic balcony seat. Lana flinches from a heart attack, and leaves in the middle of a number. As she begins her descent down the theater steps, she responds to the strains heard out in the lobby of Tony Martin's improbably melli-fluous voice singing "You Stepped Out of a Dream." The song acts as a restorative. Lana throws her shoulders back, drags her coat down the carpeted steps, and takes the steps to the beat of the music. The moment is both sublime and ridiculous, and concludes with Lana collapsing photogenically at the foot of the steps.

Garland's next film, *Life Begins for Andy Hardy* (1941), was a return—her last one—to the series as Betsy Booth. Here, she was called upon to do little but accompany Andy Hardy to New York and look on wistfully as he becomes embroiled in "big city" adventures. She recorded four songs for the film, including "America," but none were used.

The third of the Mickey-Judy musicals was also released in 1941. It was *Babes on Broadway*, and was made up of the same familiar ingredients and basically the same personnel: Busby Berkeley directing, Arthur Freed producing and contributing an occasional lyric, and Roger Edens writing special material. Where the show the kids put on in *Babes in Arms* is prematurely shut down by a hurricane, here it is halted in mid-performance when officials arrive to inform them that their theater is in a condemned building and the audience must leave. And just as in the other shows, Mickey and Judy are triumphant on Broadway in the last reel.

BABES ON BROADWAY (1941). With Mickey Rooney

Judy sings "Mary's a Grand Old Name," "Rings on My Fingers," and "How About You." Mickey does several impersonations, including one of Carmen Miranda. The finale is a large-scale minstrel show, staged by Berkeley with some spirit and imagination.

Babes on Broadway is important only as the beginning of Garland's professional relationship with director Vincente Minnelli. Freed had lured him from Broadway, hoping to nurture the young man's talent for staging and art direction. One of Minnelli's first assignments was to oversee some of Garland's musical numbers.

For Me and My Gal (1942) was a logical adjunct to Garland's War Bond tours and rallies—which were *de rigueur* for stars under MGM contract. (Fittingly, the print of this film made available for a recent screening still carries the Liberty Bond logo.) Metro's patriotic sacrifice of Garland to the war effort probably explains her reduced shooting schedule in 1942. The only other Garland film in release that year was a documentary short, *We Must Have Music*. This film explained the workings of the studio music department. To do so, MGM used, with uncharacteristic thrift, a deleted Garland production number from *Ziegfeld Girl*.

Possibly because of a confusion of aims, *For Me and My Gal* is, for the most part, rather grim. It was first of all the film debut of Gene Kelly, who had just achieved a stunning Broadway success in Rodgers and Hart's *Pal Joey*. To exploit the "innovative" ambivalence of his Pal Joey characterization—considered a giant step for the character development of musical heroes —the scriptwriters created an opportunistic vaudevillian who redeems himself in the eyes of the audience by suffering genuine remorse and doing good deeds for the remission of his sins.

The time is just before and during World War I. (It has one of those examples of movie exposition which drop like a sledge hammer: riding a train from one gig to another, Garland casually covers a dozing Kelly with a newspaper whose banner headline shrieks that the Lusitania has been sunk.) Garland, as Jo Hayden, is half of a song-and-dance team with George Murphy, as Jimmy Metcalf. Kelly plays Harry Palmer, a talented but egocentric solo performer appearing on the same bill. It's instant animosity between Garland and Kelly, but by a fluke they discover how professionally suited they are for one another. In a restaurant they work out an off-the-cuff routine to "For Me and My Gal." Also by a fluke, Murphy, playing

FOR ME AND MY GAL (1942).
As Jo Hayden

64

FOR ME AND MY GAL (1942). With Horace (Stephen) McNally, Keenan Wynn, and Gene Kelly

straight the kind of boob Ralph Bellamy kidded throughout the thirties, sees them working together through the restaurant window and steps aside so Garland can move ahead with this more talented partner.

The aspiration of every vaudeville performer is to play the Palace. When the U.S. Army threatens to frustrate this goal, Kelly places his hand on the edge of an open theatrical trunk and brings the cover down heavily on the hand in order to postpone his induction and keep the Palace booking.

Besides showcasing Kelly, the film is also intended as a tribute to vaudevillians. The dedication reads: "To one of America's great loves . . . that part of show business called 'Vaudeville'." The title number, which became a hit Decca recording, and the "Ballin' the

66

Jack" duet and Garland's torchy "After You're Gone" may be considered tributes, but the rest of the film is more funereal. Loaded plot devices conspire to put the three stars—all gone their separate ways—in the same uniform in the same room in the same European city, Paris, at the end of the film. Garland is entertaining troops with a vigorous medley of World War I songs, at the same time that soldiers Kelly and Murphy bump into each other in a corridor. All the plot's strands are untangled at once.

The film was directed by Busby Berkeley, but is nonetheless terribly bland. It could have used some of his wilder imaginings.

In 1943 Garland was back to business as usual. *Presenting Lily Mars* was originally intended by producer Joe Pasternak as a dramatic vehicle for Lana Turner, but it was refashioned as a musical for Garland. It was in keeping with the studio's policy of associating her

FOR ME AND MY GAL (1942). With Gene Kelly

PRESENTING LILY MARS (1943). With Van Heflin

GIRL CRAZY (1943). With Mickey Rooney

with pointedly nostalgic material. The source for the film was a novel by Booth Tarkington, the author of *Penrod* and *Seventeen*. It was doubly suitable for her: not only did it look back to what many liked to believe were less complicated times, but it was also the story of a small-town girl trying to break into show business. (Naturally, she succeeds and even captures producer Van Heflin.) The film was considered unremarkable by contemporary reviewers—*The New York Times* called it "glorified monotony"—but many of them excepted a charming duet Garland does with veteran actress Connie Gilchrist to "Every

Little Movement." Garland even plays Lady Macbeth's sleepwalking sequence when she tries out for a play.

When Mayer looked at the rough cut of *Lily Mars*, he judged it too subdued. He ordered Pasternak to add a more showy finish. A production number in which Garland displays the talent that enables Lily Mars to achieve stardom was written in. Her dance partner in this segment was Charles Walters, who would later direct her in *Easter Parade* and *Summer Stock*.

When the studio decided that audiences would still flock to see more of Mickey and Judy, *Girl*

Crazy (1943) was put into production. This time, Freed and Berkeley couldn't agree on a concept for the film, so Berkeley agreed to handle only the musical numbers and Norman Taurog was assigned to direct. Except for their number together in *Words and Music*, it was the last time Mickey and Judy performed together in a film.

Girl Crazy was originally the 1930 Broadway show in which Ethel Merman, in a subsidiary role, created a sensation singing "I Got Rhythm." It was filmed the following year, with Mitzi Green in the Merman role. For the 1943 version, Berkeley tried to duplicate the Merman voltage with his musical numbers. "I Got Rhythm" became the final number in the film, an elaborate, fast-stepping production in which the screen is filled with cowboy and cowgirl singers and dancers. Judy sang the Gershwin songs, "But Not For Me," "Bidin' My Time," and "Embraceable You," with delicacy and feeling.

The plot for this Mickey-Judy outing has Mickey as a high-living New York playboy forced by his father to attend an Arizona college that is short of funds. To save the school, Mickey stages a musical rodeo that is supposed to encourage applications to the school. Judy plays the dean's daughter, who enters the contest for rodeo queen. She looked charming in buckskins.

Garland's third film in 1943 was *Thousands Cheer*, another of the many star-heavy patriotic musicals produced during the war years. She made a guest appearance, singing "The Joint Is Really Jumping Down in Carnegie Hall" at a serviceman's show drummed up by inductee Gene Kelly. The film's thin plot involved Kathryn Grayson as a colonel's daughter in love with Kelly, an ex-circus performer now working for Uncle Sam.

Her next film, *Meet Me in St. Louis* (1944), began a new phase of her career, marking her passage into mature roles. As one of MGM's top critical and financial successes, it also meant that she merited even more special star treatment.

It is easy to understand the great popular success of this film at the time of its release and as a perennial favorite of moviegoers over the years. Only a curmudgeon could object to its serene, pastel-hued fantasy of home life. Again Arthur Freed was the prime mover. After reading the first installment of Sally Benson's *New Yorker* magazine reminiscences of growing up in the St. Louis of 1903 and 1904, Freed purchased the property and transported the author to Hollywood to work on a rough draft of the script. He proposed calling the film *Meet Me in St. Louis*, after the old song.

Freed liked the work of composers Ralph Blane and Hugh Martin.

70

GIRL CRAZY (1943). With Tommy Dorsey and his orchestra

MEET ME IN ST. LOUIS (1944).
As Esther Smith

They had written a bright score for *Best Foot Forward*, which Freed had just filmed. He hired them for the new film, and they wrote a group of enchanting songs which have become standards: "The Trolley Song," "Have Yourself a Merry Little Christmas" and "The Boy Next Door."

Meet Me in St. Louis was made with care, respect and affection by Vincente Minnelli. (With American GIs dispersed on either side of the Continent, it is no wonder the national appetite craved such dreams of domestic life in another era as *Life with Father* and *I Remember Mama*.) The film centered on the Smith family, idealized in all respects yet warmly believable: the stern but kind-hearted father (Leon Ames), the gentle mother (Mary Astor), four daughters (Judy Garland, Lucille Bremer, Joan Carroll, Margaret O'Brien), a son (Henry Daniels, Jr.), a crusty grandfather (Harry Davenport), and an outspoken cook (Marjorie Main).

Garland plays Esther, the second oldest of the four sisters. Whether mooning over the shy, handsome boy next door (Tom Drake), fretting about the fortunes of the family, or bursting into song, she gives a sensitive, thoughtful, unforced performance. She is confident and assured, and seems genuinely solicitous of Margaret O'Brien, playing her baby sister

MEET ME IN ST. LOUIS (1944). With Margaret O'Brien and Henry Daniels, Jr.

MEET ME IN ST. LOUIS (1944). With Lucille Bremer and Tom Drake

Tootie. She doesn't seem to mind that little Miss O'Brien, who collected a miniature Oscar for her performance in the film, just about steals the movie. Garland landed on the cover of *Life* for her performance, but Miss O'Brien won the heart of critic James Agee. Reviewing the film for *The Nation*, Agee neglected even to mention that Judy Garland was in the movie, and had to reach up for "Garbo" for an adequate point of comparison with O'Brien's performance. That young actress' performance—she was only seven at the time—is the only stray element in a basically predictable pattern.

O'Brien's performance seems studied at first, and her precision of speech is off-putting until you realize it is a legitimate facet of her

74

ghoulish character. Tootie buries her dolls and blithely masterminds a prank that causes the derailment of a trolley car. Looking at it as Tootie's movie, a viewer can see it as her progress from a seat in the front of the ice wagon to a seat next to the driver of a rig destined for the St. Louis World's Fair.

This is not to slight the rest of the picture, which glows with the richness of George Folsey's photography and the art direction of Cedric Gibbons and Lemuel Ayers. Every detail of the production was carefully planned and coordinated, from the rows of Victorian houses on the St. Louis street right on down to the bloom on Lucille Bremer's cheeks. Scene after scene works beautifully to establish a mood, a portrait of a special place and time: the famous Halloween sequence that captures childhood terrors as Tootie is chosen by friends to throw flour into the face of a neighborhood "ogre"; the Smith party at which Esther and a nightgowned Tootie do a delightful cakewalk to "Under the Bamboo Tree" and perhaps best of all, the scene in which Esther sings a hushed and tender "Have Yourself a Merry Little Christmas" to reassure her little sister about their leaving St. Louis, only to have

MEET ME IN ST. LOUIS (1944). With Mary Astor and Lucille Bremer

Tootie rush into the snow-laden yard to hysterically destroy her snowmen.

The film is committed to cheerfulness. The threatened exodus from beloved St. Louis for the financially greener fields of New York City is averted and only serves to reaffirm the family's love of its home town. The two elder Smith girls get their guys and even the girl from the East who is forecast as a villainess turns out to be a benefactress after all.

The Clock (1945) is the only dramatic film Garland made at Metro. Although Fred Zinnemann began the film, Garland couldn't get along with him and asked that he be replaced by Minnelli. It was also Minnelli's first dramatic film. The footage shot under Zinnemann was scrapped, and Minnelli began afresh. It is a simple story, simply told and persuasively played by Garland and Robert Walker. She is a secretary and he is a GI on forty-eight-hour leave. They meet in Pennsylvania Station when she trips over his outstretched legs and breaks the heel on her shoe. Animosity brings them together in the great movie tradition, but it quickly cools and becomes attraction, then affection, and then love. They marry, spend one night and morning together as a honeymoon, and he goes off to an uncertain future. Minnelli derives the maximum amount of emotion from their separation by filming it with great restraint, eschewing what is standard for this kind of scene. Garland leaves her husband at the gate, turns around, doesn't look back, and gets swallowed up in the crowd of people as the camera pulls further and further away from her.

Minnelli has commented that he was trying to make the city of New York the third character in the film. The intention is too plain—he strains to *give* character to the city instead of just discovering it. And he strikes false notes with the characters in the margins of the picture. For example, Garland's plain roommate (Ruth Brady) is painted in one broad stroke of the brush. The idea that is supposed to animate her is that she is a compulsive chatterbox who won't listen to anybody else. Her boyfriend, played by Marshall Thompson, is also trapped in the scriptwriter's idea of him. He is as pathetically silent as she is talkative.

Minnelli has said that the "beautiful screenplay" that he was handed "wouldn't work when it was filmed. The studio was planning to shelve it. It was the story of a young boy and girl who wander around New York saying banalities to cover up what they really feel; it was very difficult to do that way because the remarks would simply have

THE CLOCK (1945). With Robert Walker

THE CLOCK (1945). With Robert Walker

sounded banal to the audience anyway."* Often so much seems to be happening around the boy and girl that the film becomes unconvincing. The script is too clogged with characters. James and Lucille Gleason as an old married couple,

provide nice contrast to the uncertainty of Garland and Walker, who will probably never come to enjoy the pleasures of growing old together.

Finally, Garland and Walker are the core of the film. Both actors bring such a quiet warmth and humor to their roles that their love affair seems completely believable. Garland, in particular, appears re-

*Charles Higham and Joel Greenberg, "Vincente Minnelli," *The Celluloid Muse: Hollywood Directors Speak*, New American Library, New York, 1972, pp. 200-201.

laxed delivering her lines. The unaffected quality that made her an exceptional child actress hadn't left her. No doubt her skill as a singer and dancer carried over to the advantage of the dramatic actress. Her control over her body enables her to make the silent breakfast "ceremony" a scene of great tenderness. The newlyweds simply gaze at each other as they go through the mundane activities of pouring coffee and eating their breakfast. Her skill sustains the scene through its long silence.

Garland looked her loveliest during the middle forties. She possessed a delicacy and a dreamy quality which suggests that she is measuring reality against a romantic ideal that is constantly before her mind's eye. These aspects of Garland made her next movie so charming. It is *The Harvey Girls* (1946), and it contains one of her most appealing performances.

Following the vogue for idealized Americana started by *Oklahoma!*, the film took place in the unsettled West of the last century. It was a good idea to build the musical around the historical footnote of Fred Harvey's chain of restaurants in the West, since it called for the fetching petticoats and leg-of-mutton sleeves of the period to dress Garland and the bevy of Harvey Girl waitresses.

Garland is a Missouri girl who moves West. She is essentially the schoolmarm of the Western film, but not puritanical and therefore much easier to take. She is Susan Bradley, who makes the journey to Sandrock to be the mail order bride of H.H. Hartsey (Chill Wills). She discovers that he is the town drunk, and although he had signed the love letters, it was Ned Trent (John Hodiak), proprietor of the Alhambra saloon, who had composed them as a "joke". Besides, Hartsey's tastes run more to the mature, fulsome Sonora Cassidy (Marjorie Main), who arrives in Sandrock on the same train that brings Susan.

Her dander up, Susan begins an ongoing battle with Trent, the sort of battle which, in traditional Hollywood terms, can only end in romance. She becomes a waitress at the new Harvey restaurant, whose tidy appearance and starched, demure "nice" girls are deeply resented by the established residents of the town. Their preference is for the boozing, gambling and wenching that goes on across the street from the Harvey restaurant at the Alhambra. The film quickly establishes a conflict between "civilization" (Harvey) and civic lawlessness (the Alhambra).

To the music of a good Johnny Mercer-Harry Warren score, the conflict takes up the inevitable comic and romantic turns. Susan's fury at Trent dissolves into accep-

79

THE HARVEY GIRLS (1946).
With John Hodiak

THE HARVEY GIRLS (1946). With Selena Royle

tance after a few setbacks, the principal one being Angela Lansbury as the flamboyant, pomaded queen of the Alhambra who favors Trent. Along the way to a happy ending, the film manages some bright moments under George Sidney's direction.

Where *The Harvey Girls* goes wrong is in its multiple subplots which take the attention away from the Garland-Hodiak relationship. Not only is there a subsidiary love interest (Cyd Charisse and Kenny Baker) but there is comic relief as well (Virginia O'Brien, Ray Bol-

ger). And all the characters have solos. It is no wonder that interest is dissipated. The film is too busy.

The Harvey Girls was a success, but it is remembered chiefly for its elaborate "On the Atchison, Topeka and the Santa Fe" number which comes early in the movie. It won the Academy Award that year as the best song. It is an exciting number, the kind that large Hollywood studios can create with professional expertise. The citizens of Sandrock begin to sing the catchy tune the moment they hear the train whistle signaling its arrival,

81

THE HARVEY GIRLS (1946). With Angela Lansbury

and they don't stop singing it until the train has pulled into the station, emptied out its passengers, and moved on to the next destination. Throughout the number, the artful arrangement of swarming singers and dancers makes for a memorable musical *tour de force*.

The quiet opening, with Garland singing "In the Valley When the Evening Sun Goes Down" from the back of a moving train is also effective.

Garland's next film continued the professional association with Minnelli, whom she had married in 1945. *Ziegfeld Follies* (1946) corrals just about everybody on the MGM lot at the time who could sing or do a comic turn. It is a revue film composed of a dozen or so comic skits and musical numbers. Most of it was directed by Minnelli, but some of the non-musical sequences were handled by George Sidney, Roy Del Ruth, Lemuel Ayers, and Robert Lewis. Minnelli has written about the difficulty of directing a picture like this, citing the need to wait around for the various stars to be free from other film assignments in order to shoot the many sequences. Production dragged on for an unusually long time.

The film was enormously successful, though this is rather baffling, as it is difficult to sit through today. It is also interesting to note the contrast between the richly designed musical sequences and the nonmusical ones, which have no visual richness at all, and look like bad television.

Garland's segment, called "A Great Lady Has 'An Interview'" has inexplicably developed a reputation. Garland's long-time associates, Kay Thompson and Roger Edens, wrote special material for her, and Charles Walters gets credit for the dance direction of the segment. It is one of the few times Garland has had to perform material so blatantly unsuitable to her. The number is supposed to make fun of the condescending ways of a famous actress giving an interview to a corps of male press representatives. The "Great Lady" announces that her next film will be a "monu-

ZIEGFELD FOLLIES (1946). "A Great Lady" is interviewed.

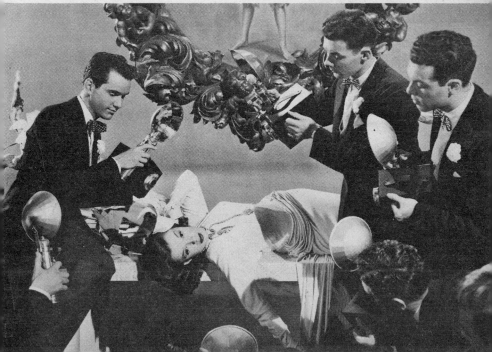

TILL THE CLOUDS ROLL BY (1946). As Marilyn Miller

mental biography" about Madame Crematon, the "discoverer" (sic) of the safety pin. She also complains that she "must always be dramatic" and not appreciated for her body. This sketch certainly conjures up Greer Garson—who Edens says turned down the opportunity to mock herself in this—but Garland's interpretation is more suggestive of Bette Davis putting on airs. Garland and her feather boa make a fine, fluttery entrance, but the rest of it is labored, clumsy satire.

Minnelli also directed Garland in her next film, *Till the Clouds Roll By* (1946), another star-laden musical revue. Their director-actress relationship must have been rare. Richard Whorf directed the overall film, but Minnelli took over the reins for Garland's two songs. Considering that Minnelli's segments stand out as the only ones in the film with any style or sophistication, it is understandable why he didn't want to turn her over to Whorf's care.

Loosely based on the career of songwriter Jerome Kern, the film is basically a medley of Kern songs attached to a wispy and improbable plot line. Kern died just before the picture went into release; from its tone one might suspect that it had been conceived as a posthumous tribute, but this was not the case. Kern was even around to act as a consultant. It is difficult to under-

stand how he countenanced Robert Walker's ludicrous, reverential portrayal. Even the casting of Walker in the part is wrong-headed as was the later casting of Mickey Rooney as Lorenz Hart in *Words and Music*.

Garland plays Marilyn Miller, the musical comedy actress of the twenties and thirties who was identified with two Kern shows: *Sally*, in which she sang "Look For the Silver Lining," and *Sunny*, in which she sang "Who?" Garland sings these two numbers in the film.

In the dramatic portion Garland as Marilyn Miller volunteers to break bad news to the novice singer (Lucille Bremer) for whom Kern has especially written "Who?" Garland must tell Bremer that she will not be singing "Who?" because the producers have judged the song too good to be tossed away on a newcomer. Garland has to deliver such venerable lines as "disappointments are a part of show business" and that the decision is "for the good of the show."

In her two musical numbers Garland comes off much better. She is given the full star treatment. The camera trails a messenger boy carrying a box of long-stemmed roses for the star, and follows him into Miller's dressing room. As she gets ready for her song, a dresser helps her out of her robe; the shot of Garland's flawless white skin and

85

TILL THE CLOUDS ROLL BY (1946). With Lucille Bremer

shoulders must have been the zenith of glamour for her. The white skin is offset by a daub of dirt artfully painted on her forehead. The camera then follows her to the stage where she sings "Look For the Silver Lining," surrounded by a roomful of dirty dishes.

Her next film, *The Pirate*, was the last collaboration with Minnelli. They were by now the parents of a daughter, Liza, born in 1946, who would inherit the Garland talent.

The Pirate (1948) is a noble experiment that simply wasn't brought off, though it does have its virtues. It was based on an S.N. Behrman play that had been a 1942

vehicle for Alfred Lunt and Lynn Fontanne. The film boasts Minnelli, Garland, Gene Kelly, and an original Cole Porter score, but it didn't measure up to expectations.

In one sense, *The Pirate* is a repetition of a typical Garland theme: a dreamy girl made to confront her dreams. Garland plays Manuela, a señorita who lives on a lush Caribbean island that is frankly out of the fairy-tale books. She focuses all her longing on the folk hero of the day—which is the early nineteeth century—Mack the Black Macoco, a notorious pirate. On an excursion with her aunt, Manuela meets Serafin, a traveling player (Kelly). She resists his attentions, but when his troupe travels to her home town, he impersonates her idol, the Black Macoco.

Kelly fulfills her fantasy of a lusty, bloodletting pirate swashbuckler. His ruse would work if the real Macoco didn't reside in the town, hidden under a veil of respectability. He is the dull, fat, middle-class mayor (Walter Slezak), to whom Manuela will be sold in marriage. The mayor has erased any trace of the notorious pirate and lives in luxury provided by the booty of his pirate years. When Kelly's impersonation almost gets

him put to death by the local authorities, the real Macoco, resentful that an imposter will get the credit and take the sentence called for by his exploits, gives himself away. Thus, Manuela is able to marry Serafin for a happy ending.

Garland's principal musical number in the film is the lusty "Mack the Black," sung while under Kelly's hypnotic spell. Performed in her most frenetic style, it has the benefit of a setting bursting with color and activity. Garland also sings "Love of My Life" to Kelly, just after she has downed

THE PIRATE (1948). With Gladys Cooper

THE PIRATE (1948). With Gene Kelly

him in a fit of rage, and the ballad "You Can Do No Wrong." Kelly is given the lavishly staged and acrobatic "Niña" (with some clever Cole Porter rhyming) and he and Garland join in the well-remembered finale, "Be a Clown," with the two cavorting infectiously in clown costumes.

There is a good deal of posturing and flourishing in *The Pirate*, especially by Kelly, but the actors' energies fail to pay off in laughs. The film is finally most memorable for some of its musical numbers and for the vividness of its deliberately unreal colors.

Garland's next film, *Easter Parade* (1948), was one of her biggest successes; like *The Wizard of Oz*, it has become a perennial television favorite. Into a standard show-business yarn, scriptwriters Sidney Sheldon and the team of Frances Goodrich and Albert Hackett wrote cues to seventeen Irving Berlin songs. It was the only time Garland appeared with Fred Astaire, and this was brought about by Gene Kelly's accident. (Making movies, especially *musical* movies, must have been especially hazardous during the late forties: Kelly broke his ankle during rehearsals for *Easter Parade*, causing Astaire to end his brief retirement by joining Garland and Ann Miller, who stepped into her role in the film when Cyd Charisse broke *her* leg. Astaire

and Garland's success at the box office prompted Betty Comden and Adolph Green to write *The Barkleys of Broadway* especially for them. Garland's illness prevented her from appearing in the film, and she was replaced by Ginger Rogers.)

Garland plays Hannah Brown, a nightclub chorine who is taken out of the chorus by Don Hewes (Astaire). Don has been deserted by his partner, Nadine Hale (Ann Miller); all one needs to know about Nadine's character is in her name. On a bet with Jonathan Harrow, III, (Peter Lawford), he picks a chorine at random (Garland: what luck!) and says he will make her into a star. The film is mainly about how he wins his bet.

Along with her Easter bonnets, Garland gets to show off her comic flair in the movie. She seems to make the opportunities even when the situation fails to provide them. For example, she and Astaire sing "Snooky Ookums," which quotes the "cutesie" love talk of a young couple. Astaire reads the lyrics straightforwardly and with a straight face. Garland, on the other hand, questions the lyrics as she sings them. She does takes and pauses half-notes before getting words out from a hesitation caused by a combination of skepticism and disbelief. She brings out the humor implicit in the song. (According to

90

THE PIRATE (1948). With Gene Kelly

EASTER PARADE (1948). With Fred Astaire

one of Garland's friends, she used to send up the inspirational "You'll Never Walk Alone" by singing it *negatively.*)

For the number "Everybody's Doing It Now" Astaire has given Hannah Brown a new name—Juanita—and a new image. He is trying to recast her in the image of his lost partner, the elegant Nadine. Garland wears an uncharacteristic costume with lots of feathers. As they go through their number, which calls for many spins and formal poses, she starts to molt. She goes through the entire number with a look of comic helplessness and anxiety on her face. On an earlier occasion, just after Don has taken her on as his partner, he tests Hannah's sex appeal by having her walk in front of him down Fifth Avenue to determine if she is able to turn a man's head. Subtle bows by Hannah get no results, but as the camera tracks behind Astaire, he is impressed by her increasing success; all heads turn. The camera returns to her and reveals why: Garland has protruded her lips and crossed her eyes.

There is a refreshing variety to

EASTER PARADE (1948). With Fred Astaire

EASTER PARADE (1948). With Dick Simmons, Ann Miller, and Fred Astaire

the crowded score: a rip-roaring duet to "When That Midnight Choo Choo Leaves for Alabam' "; the plaintive "Better Luck Next Time" and "I Wish I Were in Michigan;" the cheerful "Happy Easter" that opens the film, and the classic title song that ends it.

Easter Parade is also the film in which Garland and Astaire do the celebrated "Couple of Swells"

routine, dressed in tramp outfits. The song and the costume were later incorporated into some of Garland's concert appearances.

Ann Miller should certainly be cited for her performance as Nadine. She is the functional villainess of musical comedy, possibly the grown-up version of the role June Preisser used to play in the Mickey-Judy musicals. As a foil

94

to Garland's openness and unpretentiousness, Miller walks down Fifth Avenue on Easter Sunday with Russian wolfhounds on the leash; in case we miss the point, she turns over to her maid a dog an admirer has bestowed upon her and remarks, "It will go with my new beige suit." Fortunately, Nadine's character in no way precludes our enjoying the way she sings and dances "Shakin' the Blues Away." The song became one of Ann Miller's most famous numbers.

Perhaps an omen, *Easter Parade* is the first film in which there are discernible fluctuations in Garland's weight. In the "Alabam'" number she is chunky; for most of the rest of the film she is svelte. It was the least of many problems over which she could no longer exert control.

The Barkleys of Broadway, which was supposed to bring Garland and Astaire back together, became instead the last Astaire-Rogers film and the first of several films which Garland would either bow out of because of poor health, or which she would begin and be unable to finish.

In 1948 Garland did manage to film a guest spot in *Words and Music.* She played herself in this disastrous life story of Lorenz Hart and Richard Rodgers. Even though it is merely a guest shot, it is notable, coming, as it did, after her failure to shoot *Barkleys of Broadway.* It was the beginning of the end for her at MGM, and one of her last performances for the studio.

As Hart, Rooney gives one of his most misguided performances. Apparently, Norman Taurog, who directed, stood around while Rooney hung himself. Rooney strikes two notes in his performance. During Hart's successful early years, Rooney is as skittish as a waterbug. When he begins to have less success with his private life, he becomes sluggish and morose. It is amazing that the director, perceiving this outrageous display, permitted it. At a neighborhood theater revival of the film, an audience that accepted its dim wit, also laughed *at* Rooney's performance. Although Garland had grown up and away from *Babes*

FADE-OUT

in Arms, Rooney was still trying to get away with broad techniques that some people had found charming in an all-American teenager, but were less tolerable in a twenty-seven-year old.

Garland has two numbers. She does a duet with Rooney, "I Wish I Were in Love Again," and a solo, "Johnny One-Note." Both numbers had been written for *Babes in Arms,* but were among the songs from the original score that were dropped in the Mickey-Judy version. Both numbers are the brightest spots in the entire film. After dispensing with the nuisance of some small talk, Judy joins Mickey in the duet of "I Wish I Were in Love Again." It is one of Rodgers and Hart's most delightful songs, and Garland does wonderful things with her arms, elbows and hands as she zips through it. She looks tired around the eyes, but her manner is easy and relaxed.

Then Garland sings the whirling "Johnny One-Note," giving it all of her old verve and excitement as she sustains the long single note that is the focal point of the song. For Mickey and Judy, it was also a note of finality, marking the last

96

WORDS AND MUSIC (1948). With Mickey Rooney

time they appeared together in a film.

After a brief rest, Garland returned to full-time work with *In the Good Old Summertime* (1949), a musical remake of the studio's own 1940 film, *The Shop Around the Corner*. Ever since the success of *Meet Me in St. Louis*, MGM had been stuffing Judy into period costumes. The melody of the title song of this film is even strikingly similar to the melody of "Meet Me in St. Louis." The setting of the older

film had been contemporary Budapest. Frances Goodrich and Albert Hackett, along with Ivan Tors, were assigned to write *Summertime*, and directed to change the scene to Chicago and to move the clock back to the turn of the century. There were comparatively few script changes; the writers shifted sections of the original script around, made the shop a music shop, gave the proprietor of the shop a love interest rather than a faithless wife as in the origi-

WORDS AND MUSIC (1948). With Tom Drake and Janet Leigh

IN THE GOOD OLD SUMMERTIME (1949). With Van Johnson.

nal version, and wrote in a practically pointless subplot involving a young violinist trying for a music scholarship.

The film was a popular success —as practically all Garland films were—but it is flat and unexciting. Its story of two music-store clerks, (Garland and Van Johnson) who grate on each other by day and carry on a love affair through the mail by night, is overly familiar and loses much in Johnson's trademarked "cute" mannerisms. There is lit-

tle effort to integrate the songs into this tale. Four times during the film Garland just ups and sings. She does "Meet Me Tonight in Dreamland," "Have a Very Merry Christmas Time," "I Don't Care" and "Put Your Arms Around Me, Honey."

Her performance is engaging throughout, though it makes more demands on her as a comedienne than as a singer. She seemed to relish low comedy when given the chance to play it. Her entrance in *Summertime* is a good example.

99

IN THE GOOD OLD SUMMERTIME (1949). Singing "Play That Barbershop Chord"

Van Johnson, leaving the post office and engrossed in Garland's letter to him, knocks her to the ground as she approaches the post office to see if there is a letter from *him*. Judy's slow burn is perfectly handled as she tries to regain her maidenly composure and Johnson ineptly tries to restore her purse, her parasol, her bird (the one perched on the crown of her hat). Her parasol collapses over her head, her coiffure is devastated, and, finally, as Johnson retreats apologetically, he takes her skirt along with him.

The movie is certainly agreeable and the decor is bandbox pretty, but there is little of the distinctive quality of the earlier Garland musicals. Only two points are worth noting: the presence of Buster Keaton in a minor role—he contributes one delicious bit of pantomime when he trips and falls on S.Z. Sakall's precious Stradivarius—and the odd fact that most of *In the Good Old Summertime* takes place in a winter setting.

The film had been made while waiting for production to start on *Annie Get Your Gun*. The studio had purchased the hit show by Irving Berlin expressly for Garland, at a sum unprecedented at MGM: $700,000. Ethel Merman had performed it over one thousand times on Broadway. Production began on the film in April, 1949. Garland prerecorded the entire score (which MGM has only recently issued), and shot scenes for the film. Some photographs of wardrobe tests which Garland made for the film have only recently been published. She looks ill and exhausted and in some of the shots, completely disoriented. It certainly makes comprehensible Garland's failure to return for work after a lunch break, which led to her suspension from the studio. About a month of shooting had been completed, and one million dollars had been spent. Arthur Freed told reporters that Judy had been persistently late or absent.

After Garland went on suspension, she checked into Peter Bent Brigham Hospital in Boston for an eleven-week rest. Louis B. Mayer paid her bill. MGM borrowed Betty Hutton from Paramount to replace Garland, and began shooting from scratch. Fortunately for the studio, the film, without Judy Garland, became a big moneymaker.

Although considerable rest was advisable, Garland returned prematurely when the call came to appear in *Summer Stock* for Joe Pasternak. During her rest Garland had added some unbecoming pounds which also put years on her.

In *Summer Stock* (1950), Garland is back in the *Babes in Arms*

IN THE GOOD OLD SUMMERTIME (1949). With Buster Keaton

SUMMER STOCK (1950). With Gene Kelly and Phil Silvers

milieu—putting on a show in a barn. A bunch of city mice with theatrical aspirations overrun a small Connecticut farm. Garland plays Jane Falbury, the proprietress of the farm who is rather hostile to the frivolous show people her sister has invited to use their barn for their revue. Ultimately, she not only relents to take the lead in the show but finds romance with the troupe's director.

Judy's last film at MGM is unexceptional, but pleasant and easy to take. In spite of her nervous collapse and illness, she managed to turn in her usual effective performance. She is unquestionably *there*, from the exuberant opening song, "If You Feel Like Singing, Sing" (sung under a shower) through "Happy Harvest" (sung at the wheel of a tractor) to the finger-snapping "Get Happy" windup.

103

SUMMER STOCK (1950). With Gene Kelly

SUMMER STOCK (1950). With Phil Silvers, Hans Conreid, and Gloria DeHaven

For the third time Gene Kelly plays opposite Garland as Joe Ross, the entrepreneur of the troupe who becomes her love interest. Eddie Bracken is good in the featured part of Orville Wingait, Jane's fiancé, a papa's boy with the sniffles and blocked sinuses. Phil Silvers is also on hand in his patented role of the hero's sidekick.

Production on *Summer Stock* dragged on for six months. Garland would show up late or not show up at all. When the picture was completed, Pasternak decided that another number was needed for the finale—the show in the barn. Lighter by fifteen or twenty pounds, Garland filmed the "Get Happy" number. The drastic

105

On the set of SUMMER STOCK with Liza Minnelli

change in her appearance understandably gave rise to a rumor that the number was one deleted from a previous film. It is a jolt for the viewer to see her one moment carrying the weight that is pretty constant through the film, then emerge for one number looking like the old Judy, and then one number later be back up to her previous weight.

Garland left for another brief rest after shooting was finished, but she was abruptly summoned to replace June Allyson, who was pregnant again, in *Royal Wedding*. This was Garland's second chance to play opposite Fred Astaire, but again she couldn't make it. She walked out in the middle of a taxing scene during rehearsals, and when she failed to show up at all for a Saturday dance rehearsal with Astaire, MGM unceremoniously dropped her from the picture and replaced her with Jane Powell. Undoubtedly, Garland's mental and physical deterioration, the harsh studio ultimatum, and her unhappy private life all conspired to bring about her attempt at suicide. She tried to cut her throat with a piece of broken glass, The wound she inflicted was superficial, but it drew big headlines, and made clear to the public how ag-

gravated the "case" of Judy Garland had become. MGM announced that it was letting her go—"for her own best interests" according to the press release—and for the first time in her adult life Garland was without a job. Her marriage to Minnelli was in its last stages, and she moved out of their home to the Beverly Hills Hotel. Soon daughter Liza joined her, and they traveled to New York.

Returning to New York, she discovered that there was no demand for her. There had been not only the bad press over the suicide attempt, but studio claims—also published in the papers—that she had been the cause of inflated production costs. Studio officials characterized her as unreliable, unpredictable, and temperamental. She was a lady with time on her hands, bewildered to find herself without an overseer and on her own for the first time, taking care of Liza by herself. She had made twenty-nine feature films and put her indelible signature on dozens of songs. Now, her movie career seemed virtually over. On June 10, 1950, just a week before the events which precipitated the final rupture with MGM, she celebrated —if that is the word—her twenty-eighth birthday.

There's seldom been a time when I wasn't married to someone," Garland has written. During this respite she met Sid Luft, a former pilot, a former theatrical producer and agent, and former husband of actress Lynn Bari. He became Garland's personal manager (and, early in 1952, her husband.) It was he who advised her to launch the series of concert appearances, a four-month tour of Europe beginning with the London Palladium. For this show's finale, she appeared in a tramp outfit like the one she and Astaire had worn for "A Couple of Swells" in *Easter Parade*. Sitting at the edge of the stage and picked out by a single spotlight, she sang "Over the Rainbow"—to the hysterical approval of her audiences.

The success of these "tryouts" in Europe and the coverage they received in the press led to an invitation from Sol Schwartz, president of RKO, to repeat her foreign triumphs as a headliner at the legendary Palace theater. The Palace had ended its days as *strictly* a vaudeville house in 1932. At that time it gave way to a policy of combined vaudeville and film shows to keep up with the Radio City Music Hall which had opened that year. By 1936, however, the house had become a straight picture palace.

For the return of Garland and the Palace, the theatre was refur-

A TRIUMPHANT INTERVAL: JUDY AT THE PALACE

bished; the art collection of showman Edward F. Albee was rounded up from other theaters to decorate the lobby of the Palace.

The moment for the return of Garland was psychologically right. After taking raps on the knuckles from gossip columnists who chided her for her lack of discipline at MGM, Garland had stood in the corner long enough. It was time for a teary reconciliation.

Luft supervised the entire production. MGM personnel who had been associated with Garland were recruited for creative assignments. Charles Walters, her director on *Summer Stock* and *Easter Parade*, staged her act; Irene Sharaff designed her costumes, and Hugh Martin, composer of "The Trolley Song," accompanied her on the piano. Most of the songs Garland sang were drawn from the scores of the films she had made at Metro. In addition, the Garland presence, electric as always, was further charged by the audiences' knowledge of her stormy private life.

The management literally put down a red carpet the night of October 16, 1951, for the glittering first-night audience. An old-

108

With Sid Luft

Judy at the Palace

fashioned variety bill, including Smith and Dale and an acrobatic act, preceded Judy's half of the program.

She came onstage to an ovation, and, according to eyewitnesses, delivered a performance as intense as the audience was prepared for. Her appearance established a long-run record at the theater, and restored the personal appearance to legitimacy. Originally announced for four weeks, the run was extended twice. Tickets were expensive, and the estimated take for the Palace was $750,000 for the nineteen-week run.

At a Sunday matinee during the fourth week of the run, Judy actually gave out onstage. It was Broadway's day off, so some troupers in the audience were able to uphold the inviolate tradition that the show must go on. Vivian Blaine, appearing on Broadway in *Guys and Dolls*, ascended the stage from her orchestra seat and performed for twenty minutes; comic Jan Murray also performed for another twenty minutes. It saved the day, but the Palace was shuttered until the following Friday evening. The temporary setback inspired another ovation when Garland returned to the boards.

But nothing quite matched the effusions of the closing night audience. Even after Judy had done her encores, the audience refused to move. Someone suggested the audience sing to her, so conductor Jack Cathcart led the orchestra in "Auld Lang Syne." Halfway through it, opera star Lauritz Melchior stood up in his seat; the rest of the audience were quick to follow. They sent Judy off the stage in tears.

111

In his autobiography, Jack L. Warner writes as if he had been the instigator of the musical remake of *A Star Is Born* with Judy Garland. However, the story of that film had preoccupied several of the principals of that 1954 production long before Sid Luft, who had just formed Transcona Productions with his wife, approached Warners about bankrolling the project.

David O. Selznick had produced *A Star Is Born* in 1937 as his first independent effort. It was a prestigious film in its day, earning seven Academy Award nominations and high praise for its director, William Wellman, and its stars, Janet Gaynor and Fredric March. The script, also praised, had been revamped by Dorothy Parker, her husband Alan Campbell, and Robert Carson (with Selznick's own strong contribution) from a little-remembered 1932 film called *What Price Hollywood?*, with Constance Bennett and Lowell Sherman. *What Price Hollywood?* was produced by Selznick and directed by George Cukor, who did the Garland version in 1954.*

Even Judy Garland's interest in *A Star Is Born* went back in time. In 1942, she had played the leading

*Even in 1932, the film's story was familiar to long-time observers of the Hollywood scene. Reportedly it was based on the careers of silent-film players Marguerite de la Motte and John Bowers.

"A STAR IS BORN"

role in a "Lux Radio Theater" condensation of the script. She played opposite Walter Pidgeon and Adolphe Menjou, who recreated his film role of producer Oliver Niles.

For the 1954 Garland film, Moss Hart rewrote the script, retaining the basic story of unknown Esther Blodgett (Garland), who becomes film star Vicki Lester, only to lose her alcoholic, self-destructive husband, ex-film star Norman Maine (James Mason). Harold Arlen and Ira Gershwin wrote a batch of new songs. It was nearly ten months in production, and all of the delays cannot be attributed to Garland. Production was under way when the decision was made to shoot the film in the new CinemaScope process. (Cukor says that the long shots of the gala Hollywood event that opens the film are actually footage of the premiere of the first CinemaScope film in release—*The Robe*—at Grauman's Chinese Theatre.) As Garland's return to the screen, it was an eagerly awaited film.

In this version of *A Star Is Born*, Esther Blodgett is a singer with a small band. Norman Maine is, as they say, one of the brightest stars

A STAR IS BORN (1954). With James Mason

A STAR IS BORN (1954). Singing "Gotta Have You Go With Me"

in the Hollywood firmament, albeit one with a drinking problem. He hears her singing in a club at an early hour in the morning, after the customers have left. Recognizing in her "that little something extra" that Ellen Terry characterized as star quality, Maine convinces Esther that she is as good as he thinks she is. He brings her to the attention of Oliver Niles (Charles Bickford), arranges a screen test, and launches the career of "Vicki Lester," which the studio decides will be the new name for Esther Blodgett. As Vicki's star rises, Norman Maine's descends. Norman drinks, despairs, and finally walks into the sea, to end his wife's unbearable burden.

A Star Is Born does not reveal new facets of the Garland talent

a crucial scene because it is the one that convinces Norman that Esther has star quality, and it is the scene that must convince us as well. If the number doesn't work, *A Star Is Born* doesn't work. However, it works beautifully. It may be the single most successful musical number Garland sang in her movie career. The song is as distinctive as she is, with a superb torchy lyric, and its presentation is right, too, as Garland wrings every emotional note without lapsing into excess. There is a strikingly composed shot of Garland wiping out, in effect, the whole brass section with one downsweep of her outstretched hand. When they wrap it up, Garland punctuates the number and contributes to the realism of the scene by a ripe giggle of satisfaction for a good song well sung.

Toward the end of the movie there is another extraordinary number. In "Somewhere There's a Someone" Garland does a parody of "the production number to end all production numbers." In its simplicity, exuberance and inventiveness, it is more satisfying than the most expensive movie musical stagings that it mocks. Vicki has returned home from a day of shooting, and acts out the number for Norman. It was very carefully worked out in advance, but Garland, who sang scores of songs hundreds of times as if they were new, performs

—but for the first time this talent is given its widest range in a single role. It is her best performance because it was her most demanding part.

The film also gave her a great song: "The Man That Got Away." Late at night, alone in the deserted night club, Esther and the boys in the band are playing and singing for themselves and each other. It is

115

A STAR IS BORN (1954).
With James Mason and Tommy Noonan

A STAR IS BORN (1954). With James Mason

A STAR IS BORN (1954). Singing "Lose That Long Face" (deleted from general release prints)

it as if she's just a half beat ahead of the song. To suggest the multiple locations of an extremely lavish number, she imaginatively turns the mundane furnishings of the living room into props—a *moderne* lamp shade becomes the hat of a Chinese; a serving tray becomes a vendor's pushcart in Rio; a saltcellar and pepper mill become maracas. Garland's enthusiasm is boundless; she performs it as if extemporaneously.

A Star Is Born is best in the first half, where we discover the star quality of Esther Blodgett and then watch her be put through the Hollywood mill. The opening scene captures the excitement and absurdity of the Hollywood opening. Here it's a benefit at the Shrine Auditorium with attending celebrities, police barriers, threatening masses of fans, chauffeured limousines, klieg lights, furs, and the final ritual before a star or starlet disappears into the theater—the celebrity interview conducted by an effusive, faceless emcee. (Raw footage of the Hollywood première of *A Star Is*

Born exists; celebrities testify to the superlative quality of a film they are about to see for the first time and pass out of the gaze of the stationary camera. The impassivity of the camera, the unedited state of the footage, and the recognition—when it was viewed about fifteen years after the footage was shot—that nearly a third of the attending celebrities were already dead all contribute to the eerie quality of the film. More to the point, this Hollywood première is not discernibly different from the one parodied in the movie.)

A STAR IS BORN (1954). With James Mason and Charles Bickford

As Esther and her suicidal Norman, Judy Garland and James Mason are superb—their effectiveness *together* is the movie's strength. They demonstrate an extraordinary rapport—and Garland never had a better or stronger leading man. Yet, Mason is almost *too* strong. The character he portrays early in the picture would hardly crumble as totally as he does in the last half. His Norman needs Hollywood, but also sees through it. He is intelligent and objective, and he suggests that he has inner resources that would enable him to chuck it all

121

and survive if necessary. Because this point is so emphatically made, it is a false note when the script calls for Norman to declare to Esther, "I destroy everything I touch. You've come too late." It is possible to accept his alcoholism and his decline, but it is less easy to accept the slump in his spirits caused by a messenger boy calling him "Mr. Lester." Mason's Norman would be amused and he and Esther would probably have a fit of the giggles about it.

Another weak spot of the film is its tendency to revel in public humiliation. There is the memorable scene of the Academy Award ceremony. Just before the announcement of the winner for best actress, Vicki looks anxiously at Norman's empty chair. She rises to accept her award, and in the middle of her speech Norman makes a drunken entrance and disrupts the whole event. The TV cameras keep rolling, and from the stage Norman makes his nationally televised plea for work. He stops only after inadvertently striking his wife in the face, and she supports him off the stage. Perhaps here is the defining characteristic of soap opera—for every moment of happiness or achievement there must be a countervailing catastrophe that modifies, if it does not obliterate, happiness.

There is a similar sequence in which Jack Carson as Libby, the nasty agent who loathes Norman, confronts his old nemesis in a bar at Santa Anita. Since Norman Maine is no longer the star, Libby is free to unload the denunciations he has been waiting the entire movie to deliver. Norman swings at him, and gets knocked down for it. The crowd gathers round, misinterpreting the scene as another instance of Norman Maine's notorious drunken disorderliness. Norman, of course, climbs back up to the bar and starts drinking in earnest.

Still another scene of emotions placed on public display occurs after Norman has committed suicide, when Vicki's travail is aggravated by movie fans impervious to her suffering. She is swamped by them at Norman's funeral. As they clutch at her veil and tear it from her face, Vicki's mouth opens in a silent scream. All three of these scenes are repeated from the Janet Gaynor version. However, the Gaynor version drew its inspiration for the funeral scene from one in *What Price Hollywood?*, where the intention was completely different. In that film, the greedy fans at Constance Bennett's wedding snatch at her *bridal* veil. The bride and groom make a forced retreat to the church. The assault is meant to be amusing rather than heartrending. This transposition dramatizes the shift in emphasis.

When *A Star Is Born* opened in

A STAR IS BORN (1954). Singing "Born in a Trunk"

September, 1954, the critics heaped praise on Garland's performance, welcoming her back to full-fledged stardom. She was nominated for an Academy Award for best actress—the only time in her career—but lost out to Grace Kelly for *The Country Girl*. The day before the Oscar ceremony in 1955, Garland had given birth to Joey Luft, her second child by Sid Luft. (Lorna, her first by him, had been born in 1952.) Camera crews set up elaborate equipment in her hospital room enabling her to speak to host Bob Hope if she was the winner. According to Garland, they made speedy exits when Grace Kelly's name was called.

Without George Cukor's knowledge, Warner Bros., the distributor of the film, decided to add a long (eighteen-minute) musical number that was supposed to be a kind of screen test, a short film made by Vicki Lester. It is the famous "Born in a Trunk" sequence, and it is a compilation of old standards along with some new material written especially for the film. It is a singing star's account of her life, intended to counteract the myth of overnight success by supplanting it with a sentimental one about the struggles and false starts that precede success. It is a showcase for Garland and is inserted —to borrow a phrase—"like a block of stone" right in the middle of the picture.

The added sequence would not have been so disastrous if it hadn't, indirectly, led to another problem for the film when it went into release. It ran, originally, one hundred eighty-two minutes, excessive for exhibitors who would have to reduce the number of film showings per day, thereby cutting into box-office receipts. To appease the exhibitors clamoring for changes, Warners deleted twenty-seven minutes. Now George Cukor believes that the original negative may have been lost, and that it is impossible to see the original release version.

Nothing can bolster the cult reputation of a film like "missing" footage, and the footage of *A Star Is Born* really is missed. Most of the deletions were made in the first half—scenes showing the developing relationship of Esther and Norman. Perhaps an even more crucial excision was of the "Lose That Long Face" number which framed Esther's teary scene with Oliver Niles in her dressing room. She is in costume for the number during the scene. Garland complained that viewers seeing the painted-on freckles for the number would wonder why she had suddenly broken out in measles. The number came late in the picture, and was probably a welcome relief in the heavy second half. The song can be *heard* on the sound-track recording.

124

A STAR IS BORN (1954). As star Vicki Lester

Although Transcona Productions had made a three-picture deal with Warner Bros., no other picture was made after *A Star Is Born*. Judy, in fact, stayed away from films until 1961 when her career had another revival. The fifties were a period of comparative quiet. She made her television debut in 1955 on "The Ford Star Jubilee." This "spectacular," which inaugurated the Ford Star series, was primarily a reprise of material from her Palace show. In the next year she made her nightclub debut at Las Vegas' New Frontier Hotel.

In 1956 Garland also returned to the Palace for a run of fifteen weeks. Reviews were not as favorable this time and laryngitis forced her to miss several performances. During the run, Sol Schwartz presented her with a gold key to the star dressing room, which has since been known as the Judy Garland Room.

During this period Garland was also plagued with financial and marital problems. There were several separations and reconciliations with Luft before their permanent separation in the early sixties.

Judy did a week of concerts at the Metropolitan Opera House in New York in 1959. At this time her physical appearance was at its worst. She looked bloated and was very overweight. It is not surprising that soon afterward she had to be hospitalized with hepatitis for five months. She rested for four months after this at her home in Beverly Hills. She then flew to London, where with Luft and the three children, she spent what may well have been the quietest, most "normal" year of her life.

By the end of the year she was ready to resume work. On August 28, 1960, she was back at the Palladium singing thirty songs to the cheers of an audience of over two thousand people. This appearance was followed by a tour of the English provinces, and two dates at the Palais de Chaillot Theatre in Paris. When she returned to London, a new man came into her life. Freddie Fields was striking out on his own as an agent and personal manager after being with the Music Corporation of America. Fields was interested in handling only "a select few clients." Garland became one of them.

With Fields her career revived briefly. Judy had filed suit against the Columbia Broadcasting System for violation of contract; it had dragged on for three years. Fields settled it, and then arranged for a single appearance on the network. He also got her signed for a small guest role in Stanley Kramer's *Judgment at Nuremberg* (1961); it would be her first film since 1954. Most important Fields booked her for a sixteen-city concert tour, including New York's Carnegie Hall. That concert, on the evening of April 23, 1961, has become theatrical history. To the audience of vastly enthusiastic Judy Garland fans, she sang twenty-six songs. A two-record album preserves the evening and the excitement in the

WHAT BECOMES A LEGEND MOST?

air. Audience and entertainer enjoyed a rapport that was practically unprecedented. The impact of that evening revived Garland's status as a legend. The recording of the concert became the first two-record set to sell over a million copies. Judy went on to the remaining cities booked for the tour and duplicated her success in each of them.

For Judy's return to the screen in *Judgment at Nuremberg,* she played a guilt-ridden German haus frau in this Stanley Kramer film on the theme of "responsibility."

The film was based on a "Playhouse 90" television production that had received wide attention. Abby Mann expanded his own script for the film version. It starred an extraordinary group of major players: Spencer Tracy, Burt Lancaster, Richard Widmark, Marlene Dietrich, and Maximilian Schell. Garland and Montgomery Clift both took small but important roles.

The film is a dramatization of one phase of the Nuremberg trials of 1948 in which German judges are brought to justice for their support of Hitler. Tracy is the trial's Chief Justice, Widmark the prosecuting attorney, and Schell the defense at-

127

JUDGMENT AT NUREMBERG (1961). As Irene Hoffman

torney. (Lancaster is the most unbending German general— Dietrich, the widow of a German officer.) In the courtroom Garland takes the stand for a climactic scene in which she testifies that a Jewish man had been falsely accused of intimacy with her, an Aryan. The man had been executed because of the charge, and the frightened woman had not spoken up to protest the accusation. Under the questioning of the defense attorney (Schell), she breaks down. Garland was at her most mannered and neurotic in this sequence. The Academy of Motion Picture Arts and Sciences nonetheless nominated her for an Oscar for the best supporting actress that year.

Garland's next film work was for a feature-length cartoon called *Gay Purr-ee* (1962). Judy did the songs and dialogue for an animated sex kitten named Mewsette. It gave Judy the chance to perform more songs by her lifelong associates, Harold Arlen and E.Y. Harburg.

JUDGMENT AT NUREMBERG (1961). With Richard Widmark

A CHILD IS WAITING (1963). As Jean Hansen

A CHILD IS WAITING (1963). With Burt Lancaster

Her next film was another Stanley Kramer drama with "serious" content. He produced *A Child Is Waiting* (1963) with John Cassavetes as director. The film was also another expansion by Abby Mann of his own teleplay. The 1957 television drama had starred Pat Hingle in the role played in the film by Burt Lancaster.

Garland plays an unmarried woman "in her thirties" who joins the staff of a private school for mentally retarded children. She wants to achieve a sense of usefulness in the world. The woman makes an adjustment to the realities of life for the children in her care, and comes to accept the kind of small triumph that is possible for these children.

131

I COULD GO ON SINGING (1963). With Dirk Bogarde and Gregory Phillips

Although this is the essential drama of the film, the scriptwriter was also interested in presenting the plight of retarded children to the American public. One can't fault him for that, but it doesn't make for much of a film. Wherever he saw an opportunity, Mann crammed "information" into the script. We are told that five million Americans suffer from mental retardation. "It happened to the sister of a president of the United States," Lancaster tells Garland, alluding to a sister of President John Kennedy. And later he preaches to her: "It's not what you can do for these children; it's what they can do for you."

It is not much of a part for Garland, but she plays it sincerely. As Jean Hansen, she is hired by at the private school as an instructor in music. She takes an unprofessional special interest in one of the boys, a borderline case. This involves her in a struggle with Dr. Clark (Lancaster) about the way the school should be run—the stern approach versus a more personal involvement. Her concern for the young boy causes her to trespass into the boy's life. His parents never visit him, and he waits futilely every visiting day for them to arrive. Jean invents a story about the boy's failing health, and tricks the parents into coming to see the child.

For most of the film her part is that of an observer. She must look concerned, sympathetic and aware of her helplessness in alleviating the plight of the retarded children. Garland also doesn't look her best. She is top-heavy, and the makeup job on her seems only to preserve the look of dissipation. She is carrying the unattractive weight that she would shed for the television series in the next year.

I Could Go On Singing (1963) was Garland's last film appearance The team that wrote her songs for the movie that propelled her to stardom, Harold Arlen and "Yip" Harburg, also contributed the title song to this film. It is in no respect the kind of *tour de force* that should have capped the movie career of this musical star. Basically a drama rather than a musical, and a tired drama at that, it has a standard tear-jerking script, and one wonders why Garland chose to do it. Her love of London, where most of the film was shot, may have been one consideration. The casting of reputable Dirk Bogarde as her co-star may have also made the project sound more viable. Judy acquits herself well enough, though she doesn't look her best. The heavy lipstick makeup does produce an almost satanic curl to her lips that is perversely appealing.

Judy plays a role with autobiographical elements. She is Jennie

*I COULD GO
ON SINGING (1963)
As Jennie Bowman*

Bowman, a famous American singer making a seven-country European tour. In London for an engagement at the Palladium, she looks up a former lover (Bogarde) and the son (Gregory Phillips) she bore him. Because Jennie's career was most important to her, she relinquished the child, now about thirteen, to his father. He returned to England, married his childhood sweetheart and raised the boy as their adopted son. With the wife now dead, Jennie wants to see the boy, and then she decides to take him away from his father. The resolution, implied in the title of the film for its British release—*The Lonely Stage*—has the boy choosing to stay with his father rather than risk the uncertainty of life with Jennie. The choice makes it possible for Garland to sing her last screen song, "I Could Go On Singing," the finale of the picture.

Because this is a British film, it was made with the well-known British restraint. The boy, hearing the inevitable revelation about his birth, behaves with stalwart manliness. What should be the dramatic highlight, the boy delivering his decision to his mother, is handled elliptically. We see Bogarde telling the boy that it is his decision to make, and then we see Garland suffering what we infer is the aftermath of her hearing of his choice to stay with the father. She is recuperating in an emergency clinic where she's been taken after a drunk.

This emotional binge has also made her late for another concert appearance. Bogarde gets her back to the theater, where an audience has been waiting restlessly for an hour. Her manager (Jack Klugman) is overwrought and estimates that it will take her at least another forty-five minutes to dress. It is at this point that Garland takes over.

She steps out onto the stage, as is, and turns on the legendary Garland magic to conciliate and charm the betrayed and hostile audience. There are jeers and shouts and a few challenging questions from the audience. "Where've you been?" one member asks. "Oh, I've been having a wild time," she answers. With no nonsense, she stomps about the stage, rolling up her sleeves and conveying an impression of getting down to business. Another member of the audience wants to know where she got the fur she is discarding. "Something I shot," she explains. Then she impatiently motions for the stagehands ("They must be asleep back there!") to part the curtains so that she can get the show on the road. It's a herculean feat, but Garland convinces that she would be able to seduce an audience back to her. She starts to sing "I Could Go On Singing" and

136

On her television show

On her television show
with Andy Williams

With fourth husband
Mark Herron

the audience listens, enraptured.

In the film Garland also sings "Hello, Bluebird," "It Never Was You," and "By Myself." When she visits her son at his boarding school, she joins him and several other boys backstage after a performance of *H.M.S. Pinafore* in an impromptu singing of "I Am the Monarch of the Sea."

The following year Garland was signed by CBS to do a television series. Garland taped twenty-six hour segments, but the show was given an impossible time slot opposite one of television's most popular and durable programs, the Western series, *Bonanza*. The program was also beset by problems, with frequent changes in personnel. For the first taping Judy insisted on Mickey Rooney as her guest.

After the failure of this show, Judy did a concert tour of Australia. In Melbourne life didn't imitate art: when she arrived one hour late for a concert, she couldn't appease the hostile crowd of seventy thousand, and after forty-five minutes, Judy strode off the stage.

In 1965 she and her daughter Liza did a concert together at the London Palladium. The event was set for one performance only. It sold out immediately. Disappointed fans clamored so loudly that a second concert was arranged, which also sold out.

During her last years Garland also took younger husbands. She was married twice in the sixties, briefly to Mark Herron, an actor several years her junior, and then to Mickey Deans, who was with her when she died. (When Judy invited Liza to her fifth wedding, Liza declined, saying, "Sorry I can't make this one, but I promise you I'll come to your next.")

Judy spent the last months of her life primarily in London, where she and Deans had taken up residence, and on the Continent, where she made some concert appearances. Her last public performance was a concert in Copenhagen.

But Garland looked very bad at this time. Thin to the point of emaciation and very fragile, she looked like some kind of exotic bird. The years of living on pills caught up with her on June 22, 1969. After spending a routine day, she and Deans retired early. The next morning he awoke to find her dead in the bathroom. The cause of death was an "accidental overdose" of sleeping pills. She was forty-seven years old.

An estimated twenty thousand people waited four hours to file past the corpse of Judy Garland when she lay in state at a Manhattan funeral parlor. An entire block was cordoned off to contain the crush of people, and the funeral home was kept open throughout

140

With fifth husband Mickey Deans

the night in order to permit more people to pay their last respects.

It was a comparatively early death, but as Judy Garland said of herself, she had crowded two lives into her one. And certainly her achievement, which lives on in the films and recordings, was enough for several people.

BIBLIOGRAPHY

Carson, Saul. "Judy Garland," *The Lonely Beauties*. New York, Popular Library, 1971.

Crowther, Bosley. *Hollywood Rajah: The Life and Times of Louis B. Mayer*. New York, Holt, Rinehart and Winston, 1960.

_____. *The Lion's Share: The Story of an Entertainment Empire*. New York; E. P. Dutton, 1957.

Deans, Mickey and Pinchot, Ann. *Weep No More, My Lady*. New York, Hawthorn, 1972.

Dickens, Homer. "Judy Garland," *Film Careers*, March, 1964.

Galling, Dennis Lee. "Arthur Freed," *Films in Review*, November, 1964.

_____. "Vincente Minnelli," *Films in Review*, March, 1964.

Garland, Judy. "The Plot Against Judy Garland," *Ladies Home Journal*, August, 1967.

_____, as told to Joe Hyams. "The Real Me," *McCall's*, April, 1957.

_____. "There'll Always be an Encore," *McCall's*, January and February, 1964.

Goode, James. "Judy," *Show Business Illustrated*, October 31, November 14 and November 28, 1961.

Higham, Charles and Greenberg, Joel. "George Cukor" and "Vincente Minnelli," *The Celluloid Muse: Hollywood Directors Speak*. New York; New American Library, 1972.

Johnson, Albert. "Conversation with Roger Edens," *Sight and Sound*, Spring, 1958.

Morella, Joe and Epstein, Edward. *Judy: The Films and Career of Judy Garland*. New York, Citadel Press, 1969.

Nagle, Doreen, editor. *Judy Garland: A Special Tribute*. New York, Skywald Publishing, 1969.

Parish, James Robert and Bowers, Ronald L. *The Golden Era: The MGM Stock Company*. New Rochelle, New York, Arlington House, 1973.

Powdermaker, Hortense. *Hollywood: The Dream Factory*. Boston, Little, Brown, 1950.

Rooney, Mickey. *i.e. An Autobiography*. New York, G.P. Putnam's Sons, 1965.

Rosterman, Robert. "Judy Garland," *Films in Review*, April, 1962.

145

Siegel, Joel. "The Pirate," *Film Heritage*, Fall, 1971.

Smith, Milburn, ed. "Judy Garland and Mickey Rooney," *Screen Greats*. New York; Barven Publications, 1972.

Spitzer, Marian. *The Palace*. New York, Atheneum, 1969.

Steiger, Brad. *Judy Garland*. New York, Ace Publishing, 1969.

Thomas, Lawrence B. *The MGM Years*. New York, Columbia House, 1972.

Thomas, Tony and Terry, Jim, with Berkeley, Busby. *The Busby Berkeley Book*. Greenwich, Connecticut, New York Graphic Society, 1973.

Thomey, Tedd. "Hollywood Suicide," in *Hollywood Confidential*. New York; Pyramid Books, 1967.

Torme, Mel. *The Other Side of the Rainbow: With Judy Garland on the Dawn Patrol*. New York, William Morrow, 1970.

Vallance, Tom. *The American Musical*. New York, A.S. Barns, 1970.

Zierold, Norman J. "The True Judy," in *The Child Stars*. New York, Coward-McCann, 1965.

THE FILMS OF JUDY GARLAND

The director's name follows the release date. A (c) following the release date indicates that the film was in color. Sp indicates screenplay and b/o indicates based on.

1. EVERY SUNDAY. One-reel. MGM, 1936. *Felix E. Feist.* Sp: Mauri Grashin. Cast: Deanna Durbin.

2. PIGSKIN PARADE. 20th Century-Fox, 1936. *David Butler.* Sp: Harry Tugend, Jack Yellen and William Conselman, b/o story by Arthur Sheekman, Nat Perrin and Mark Kelly. Cast: Stuart Erwin, Patsy Kelly, Jack Haley, The Yacht Club Boys, Johnny Downs, Betty Grable, Arline Judge, Dixie Dunbar, Anthony (Tony) Martin.

3. BROADWAY MELODY OF 1938. MGM, 1937. *Roy Del Ruth.* Sp: Jack McGowan, b/o story by McGowan and Sid Silvers. Cast: Robert Taylor, Eleanor Powell, George Murphy, Binnie Barnes, Sophie Tucker, Buddy Ebsen, Charles I. Gorin, Raymond Walburn, Robert Benchley.

4. THOROUGHBREDS DON'T CRY. MGM, 1937. *Alfred E. Green.* Sp: Lawrence Hazard, b/o story by Eleanore Griffin and J. Walter Ruben. Cast: Mickey Rooney, Sophie Tucker, C. Aubrey Smith, Ronald Sinclair, Forrester Harvey.

5. EVERYBODY SING. MGM, 1938. *Edwin L. Marin.* Sp: Florence Ryerson and Edgar Allan Woolf, additional dialogue by James Gruen. Cast: Allan Jones, Fanny Brice, Billie Burke, Reginald Owen, Lynne Carver, Reginald Gardiner, Henry Armetta, Monty Woolley.

6. LISTEN, DARLING. MGM, 1938. *Edwin L. Marin.* Sp: Elaine Ryan and Anne Morrison Chapin, b/o story by Katherine Brush. Cast: Freddie Bartholomew, Mary Astor, Walter Pidgeon, Alan Hale, Scotty Beckett, Gene Lockhart, Barnett Parker, Byron Foulger.

147

7. LOVE FINDS ANDY HARDY. MGM, 1938. *George B. Seitz.* Sp: William Ludwig, b/o stories by Vivien R. Bretherton and characters created by Aurania Rouverol. Cast: Lewis Stone, Mickey Rooney, Cecilia Parker, Ann Rutherford, Lana Turner, Fay Holden, Don Castle, Gene Reynolds, Marie Blake, George Breakston.

8. THE WIZARD OF OZ. MGM, 1939. (c). *Victor Fleming.* Sp: Noel Langley and Florence Ryerson, and Edgar Allan Woolf, b/o story by L. Frank Baum. Cast: Frank Morgan, Ray Bolger, Bert Lahr, Jack Haley, Billie Burke, Margaret Hamilton, Clara Blandick, Charley Grapewin, Pat Walshe, Singer's Midgets.

9. BABES IN ARMS. MGM, 1939. *Busby Berkeley.* Sp: Jack McGowan and Kay Van Riper, b/o play by Richard Rodgers and Lorenz Hart. Cast: Mickey Rooney, Charles Winninger, Guy Kibbee, June Preisser, Grace Hayes, Betty Jaynes, Douglas McPhail, Rand Brooks, Leni Lynn, John Sheffield, Henry Hull, Barnett Parker, Ann Shoemaker, Margaret Hamilton.

10. ANDY HARDY MEETS DEBUTANTE. MGM, 1940. *George B. Seitz.* Sp: Annalee Whitmore and Thomas Seller, b/o characters created by Aurania Rouverol. Cast: Lewis Stone, Mickey Rooney, Cecilia Parker, Fay Holden, Ann Rutherford, Diana Lewis, George Breakston, Sara Haden, George Lessey, Harry Tyler.

11. STRIKE UP THE BAND. MGM, 1940. *Busby Berkeley.* Sp: John Monks, Jr., and Fred Finklehoffe. Cast: Mickey Rooney, Paul Whiteman, June Preisser, William Tracy, Larry Nunn, Margaret Early, Ann Shoemaker, Francis Pierlot, Virginia Brissac.

12. LITTLE NELLIE KELLY. MGM, 1940. *Norman Taurog.* Sp: Jack McGowan, b/o musical comedy by George M. Cohan. Cast: George Murphy, Charles Winninger, Douglas McPhail, Arthur Shields, James Burke, Robert Homans, Thomas P. Dillon.

13. ZIEGFELD GIRL. MGM, 1941. *Robert Z. Leonard.* Sp: Marguerite Roberts and Sonya Levien, b/o story by William Anthony McGuire. Cast: James Stewart, Hedy Lamarr, Lana Turner, Tony Martin, Jackie Cooper, Ian Hunter, Charles Winninger, Edward Everett Horton, Philip Dorn, Paul Kelly, Eve Arden, Dan Dailey, Al Shean.

14. LIFE BEGINS FOR ANDY HARDY. MGM, 1941. *George B. Seitz.* Sp: Agnes Christine Johnston, b/o characters created by Aurania Rouverol. Cast: Mickey Rooney, Lewis Stone, Fay Holden, Ann Rutherford, Sara Haden, Patricia Dane, Ray McDonald, George Breakston, Pierre Watkin.

15. BABES ON BROADWAY. MGM, 1941. *Busby Berkeley.* Sp: Fred Finklehoffe and Elaine Ryan, b/o story by Finklehoffe. Cast: Mickey Rooney, Fay Bainter, Virginia Weidler, Ray McDonald, Richard Quine, Donald Meek, James Gleason, Emma Dunn, Frederick Burton, Alexander Woollcott, Donna Adams (Donna Reed), Cliff Clark.

16. FOR ME AND MY GAL. MGM, 1942. *Busby Berkeley.* Sp: Richard Sherman, Fred Finklehoffe and Sid Silvers, b/o story by Howard Emmett Rogers. Cast: George Murphy, Gene Kelly, Marta Eggerth, Ben Blue, Richard Quine, Keenan Wynn, Horace (Stephen) McNally, Lucille Norman.

17. PRESENTING LILY MARS. MGM, 1943. *Norman Taurog.* Sp: Richard Connell and Gladys Lehman, b/o novel by Booth Tarkington. Cast: Van Heflin, Fay Bainter, Richard Carlson, Spring Byington, Marta Eggerth, Connie Gilchrist, Leonid Kinskey, Ray McDonald, Charles Walters.

18. GIRL CRAZY. MGM, 1943. *Norman Taurog.* Sp: Fred Finklehoffe, b/o musical by Guy Bolton and Jack McGowan. Cast: Mickey Rooney, Gil Stratton, Robert E. Strickland, Rags Ragland, June Allyson, Nancy Walker, Guy Kibbee, Frances Rafferty, Howard Freeman, Henry O'Neill.

19. THOUSANDS CHEER. MGM, 1943. (c). *George Sidney.* Sp: Paul Jarrico and Richard Collins, b/o their story "Private Miss Jones." Cast: Kathryn Grayson, Gene Kelly, Mary Astor, Jose Iturbi, John Boles, Dick Simmons, Ben Blue. Guest Stars: Mickey Rooney, Red Skelton, Eleanor Powell, Ann Sothern, Lucille Ball, Virginia O'Brien, Lena Horne.

20. MEET ME IN ST. LOUIS. MGM, 1944. (c). *Vincente Minnelli.* Sp: Irving Brecher and Fred Finklehoffe, b/o stories by Sally Benson. Cast: Margaret O'Brien, Mary Astor, Lucille Bremer, Tom Drake, Marjorie Main, Leon Ames, Harry Davenport, June Lockhart, Henry Daniels, Jr., Joan Carroll, Hugh Marlowe, Chill Wills.

21. THE CLOCK. MGM, 1945. *Vincente Minnelli*. Sp: Robert Nathan and Joseph Schrank, b/o story by Paul Gallico and Pauline Gallico. Cast: Robert Walker, James Gleason, Keenan Wynn, Marshall Thompson, Lucille Gleason, Ruth Brady.

22. THE HARVEY GIRLS. MGM, 1946. (c). *George Sidney*. Sp: Edmund Beloin, Nathaniel Curtis, Samson Raphaelson, Harry Crane, and James O'Hanlon, story by Eleanore Griffin and William Rankin, b/o book by Samuel Hopkins Adams. Cast: John Hodiak, Ray Bolger, Preston Foster, Virginia O'Brien, Angela Lansbury, Marjorie Main, Chill Wills, Kenny Baker, Selena Royle, Cyd Charisse, Ruth Brady.

23. ZIEGFELD FOLLIES. MGM, 1946. (c). *Vincente Minnelli*. Sequences also directed by George Sidney, Robert Lewis, Lemuel Ayers, and Roy Del Ruth. Cast: Fred Astaire, Lucille Ball, Lucille Bremer, Fanny Brice, Kathryn Grayson, Lena Horne, Gene Kelly, James Melton, Victor Moore, Red Skelton, Esther Williams, William Powell.

24. TILL THE CLOUDS ROLL BY. MGM, 1946. (c). *Richard Whorf*. Garland's numbers directed by Vincente Minnelli. Sp: Myles Connolly and Jean Holloway, story by Guy Bolton, adapted by George Wells, b/o the life and music of Jerome Kern. Cast: June Allyson, Lucille Bremer, Kathryn Grayson, Van Heflin, Lena Horne, Van Johnson, Tony Martin, Dinah Shore, Frank Sinatra, Robert Walker.

25. THE PIRATE. MGM, 1948. (c). *Vincente Minnelli*. Sp: Albert Hackett and Frances Goodrich, b/o play by S.N. Behrman. Cast: Gene Kelly, Walter Slezak, Gladys Cooper, Reginald Owen, George Zucco, Nicholas Brothers, Lola Deem.

26. EASTER PARADE. MGM, 1948. (c). *Charles Walters*. Sp: Sidney Sheldon, Albert Hackett and Frances Goodrich, b/o story by Hackett and Goodrich. Cast: Fred Astaire, Peter Lawford, Ann Miller, Clinton Sundberg, Jules Munshin, Jeni LeGon, Jimmy Bates, Richard Beavers, Dick Simmons.

27. WORDS AND MUSIC. MGM, 1948. (c). *Norman Taurog*. Sp: Fred Finklehoffe, story by Guy Bolton and Jean Holloway, adaptation by Ben Feiner, Jr., b/o the lives of Richard Rodgers and Lorenz Hart. Cast: Mickey Rooney, Perry Como, Ann Sothern, Tom Drake, Betty Garrett, Janet Leigh. Guest Stars: June Allyson, Gene Kelly, Lena Horne, Mel Torme.

28. IN THE GOOD OLD SUMMERTIME. MGM, 1949. (c). *Robert Z. Leonard.* Sp: Albert Hackett, Frances Goodrich and Ivan Tors; from a screenplay by Samson Raphaelson and a play by Miklos Laszlo. Cast: Van Johnson, S.Z. "Cuddles" Sakall, Spring Byington, Clinton Sundberg, Buster Keaton, Marcia Van Dyke.

29. SUMMER STOCK. MGM, 1950. (c). *Charles Walters.* Sp: George Wells and Sy Gomberg, b/o story by Gomberg. Cast: Gene Kelly, Eddie Bracken, Gloria DeHaven, Marjorie Main, Phil Silvers, Ray Collins, Nita Bieber, Carleton Carpenter, Hans Conreid.

30. A STAR IS BORN. Warner Bros., 1954. (c). *George Cukor.* Sp: Moss Hart, b/o screenplay by Dorothy Parker, Alan Campbell and Robert Carson, from a story by William A. Wellman and Carson. Cast: James Mason, Jack Carson, Charles Bickford, Tom Noonan, Lucy Marlow, Amanda Blake, Irving Bacon, Hazel Shermet, Joan Shawlee.

31. PEPE. Columbia, 1960. (c). *George Sidney.* Sp: Dorothy Kingsley and Claude Binyon, story by Leonard Spigelgass and Sonya Levien, b/o play by L.Bush-Fekete. Cast: Cantinflas, Shirley Jones, Dan Dailey, and the voice of Judy Garland.

32. JUDGMENT AT NUREMBERG. Kramer-United Artists, 1961. *Stanley Kramer.* Sp: Abby Mann, b/o his own teleplay. Cast: Spencer Tracy, Burt Lancaster, Richard Widmark, Marlene Dietrich, Maximilian Schell, Montgomery Clift.

33. GAY PURR-EE. Warner Bros.-UPA, 1962. (c). *Abe Levitow.* Sp: Dorothy and Chuck Jones. An animated cartoon featuring the voices of Judy Garland, Robert Goulet, Red Buttons, Hermione Gingold, Paul Frees, Morey Amsterdam, Mel Blanc.

34. A CHILD IS WAITING. Kramer-United Artists, 1963. *John Cassavetes.* Sp: Abby Mann, b/o his own story. Cast: Burt Lancaster, Gena Rowlands, Steven Hill, Paul Stewart. Gloria McGehee, Lawrence Tierney, Bruce Ritchey, John Marley, Bill Mumy, John Walker, Elizabeth Wilson, Barbara Pepper, and the Children.

35. I COULD GO ON SINGING. United Artists, 1963. (c). *Ronald Neame.* Sp: Mayo Simon, b/o story by Robert Dozier. Cast: Dirk Bogarde, Jack Klugman, Gregory Phillips, Aline MacMahon, Pauline Jameson, Jeremy Burnham.

INDEX

153

154

155

157

ABOUT THE AUTHOR
James Juneau has written reviews as a staff member of the trade magazine, *The Independent Film Journal*. He has also done instructive time in the publicity department of American International Pictures.

ABOUT THE EDITOR

Ted Sennett is the author of *Warner Brothers Presents*, a survey of the great Warner films of the Thirties and Forties, and of *Lunatics and Lovers*, on the years of the "screwball" movie comedy. He has also written about films for magazines and newspapers. He lives in New Jersey with his wife and three children.